The Horologicon

THE ELEMENTS OF
ELOQUENCE
How to Turn the
Perfect English Phrase

MARK FORSYTH

ICON

This edition published in the UK in 2016 by
Icon Books Ltd, Omnibus Business Centre,
39–41 North Road, London N7 9DP
email: info@iconbooks.com
www.iconbooks.com

First published in the UK in 2013 by Icon Books Ltd

Sold in the UK, Europe and Asia
by Faber & Faber Ltd, Bloomsbury House,
74–77 Great Russell Street,
London WC1B 3DA or their agents

Distributed in the UK, Europe and Asia
by Grantham Book Services,
Trent Road, Grantham NG31 7XQ

Distributed in Australia and New Zealand
by Allen & Unwin Pty Ltd,
PO Box 8500, 83 Alexander Street,
Crows Nest, NSW 2065

Distributed in South Africa
by Jonathan Ball, Office B4, The District,
41 Sir Lowry Road, Woodstock 7925

Distributed in India
by Penguin Books India,
7th Floor, Infinity Tower – C, DLF Cyber City,
Gurgaon 122002, Haryana

ISBN: 978-178578-172-8

Typeset in Minion by Marie Doherty
Printed and bound in the UK by Clays Ltd, St Ives plc

Contents

Acknowledgements

I would like to bow down in thanks and prose to Jane Seeber for her indefatigable aid.

For the last year, I have been unbearable company. My only question to friend or foe alike has been 'Can you think of any famous phrases that follow this particular structure?' Many people have helped, but I can't exactly remember who. My thanks should probably go, in no particular order, to Jane Seeber, Andrea Coleman, Rob Colvile, Nick Popper, John Goldsmith, Michael Mellor, Hilary Scott, Adrian Hornsby, James Forsyth, Allegra Stratton, Alicia Roberts, Nick Roberts, my parents, Laura Humble, Simon Blake, Alister Whitford, Jeremy Large, Chris Mann, Claire Bodanis, Julia Kingsford, Ed Howker and anybody else whom I have rudely forgotten in my absence of mind.

About the author

MARK FORSYTH is a writer whose books have made him one of the UK's best-known commentators on words and the English language. *The Etymologicon* was a *Sunday Times* #1 Bestseller and BBC Radio 4 'Book of the Week', as was his second book *The Horologicon*. He writes the Inky Fool blog and has contributed articles to the *Guardian, Daily Telegraph, Spectator, New York Times* and *Wall Street Journal* among others. He lives in Clerkenwell, London.

Does an 'explanation' make it any less impressive?

Wittgenstein, *Remarks on Frazer's Golden Bough*

—⊶⊷—

On Cooking Blindfolded

Shakespeare was not a genius. He was, without the distant shadow of a doubt, the most wonderful writer who ever breathed. But not a genius. No angels handed him his lines, no fairies proofread for him. Instead, he learnt techniques, he learnt tricks, and he learnt them well.

Genius, as we tend to talk about it today, is some sort of mysterious and combustible substance that burns brightly and burns out. It's the strange gift of poets and pop stars that allows them to produce one wonderful work in their early twenties and then nothing. It is mysterious. It is there. It is gone.

This is, if you think about it, a rather odd idea. Nobody would talk about a doctor or an accountant or a taxi driver who burnt out too fast. Too brilliant to live long. Pretty much everyone in every profession outside of professional athletics gets better as they go along, for the rather obvious reason that they learn and they practise. Why should writers be different?

Shakespeare wasn't different. Shakespeare got better and better and better, which was easy because he started badly, like most people starting a new job.

Nobody is quite sure which is Shakespeare's first play, but the contenders are *Love's Labour's Lost*, *Titus Andronicus*, and *Henry VI Part 1*. Do not, dear reader, worry if you have not read those plays. Almost nobody has, because, to be utterly frank, they're not very good. To be precise about it, there isn't a single memorable line in any of them.

Now, for Shakespeare, that may seem rather astonishing. He was, after all, the master of the memorable line. But the first line of Shakespeare that almost anybody knows is in *Henry VI Part 2*, when one revolting peasant says to another: 'The first thing we do, let's kill all the lawyers.' In *Part 3* there's a couple more – 'I can smile, and murder while I smile'. And each successive play has more and more and more great lines until you work up through *Much Ado* and *Julius Caesar* (1590s) to *Hamlet* and *King Lear* (1600s).

Shakespeare got better because he learnt. Now some people will tell you that great writing cannot be learnt. Such people should be hit repeatedly on the nose until they promise not to talk nonsense any more. Shakespeare was taught how to write. He was taught it at school. Composition (in Latin) was the main part of an Elizabethan education. And, importantly, you had to learn the figures of rhetoric.

Professionally, Shakespeare wrote in English. And for that he learnt and used the figures of rhetoric in English. This was easy, as Elizabethan London was crazy for rhetorical figures. A chap called George Puttenham had a bestseller in 1589 with his book on them (that's about the year of Shakespeare's first play). And that was just following on from Henry Peacham's *The Garden of Eloquence*, which had come out a decade earlier. Book after book was published, all about the figures of rhetoric. So I should probably explain what the figures of rhetoric are.

Rhetoric is a big subject. It consists of the whole art of persuasion. The lot. It includes logic (or the kind of sloppy logic most people understand, called enthymemes), it includes speaking loudly and clearly, and it includes working out what topics to talk about. Anything to do with persuasion is rhetoric, right down to the *argumentum ad baculum*, which means *threatening somebody with a stick until they agree with you*. One minuscule part of this massive subject is the figures of rhetoric, which are the techniques for making a single phrase striking and memorable just by altering the wording. Not by saying something different, but by saying something in a different way. They are the formulas for producing great lines.

These formulas were thought up by the Ancient Greeks and then added to by the Romans. As Shakespeare set to work England was busy having the Renaissance (everybody else had had the Renaissance a century or so before, and we were running late). So the classical works on rhetoric were dug out, translated and adapted for use in English. But it wasn't the enthymemes or the topics or even the baculums that the English liked. We loved the figures. The 'flowers of rhetoric' as they were called (hence *The Garden of Eloquence*), because, as a nation, we were at the time rather obsessed with poetry.

So Shakespeare learnt and learnt and got better and better, and his lines became more and more striking and more and more memorable. But most of his great and famous lines are simply examples of the ancient formulas. 'I can smile, and murder while I smile' was not handed to Shakespeare by God. It's just an example of diacope.

So why, you may be asking, were you not taught the figures of rhetoric at school? If they make a chap write as well as Shakespeare, shouldn't we be learning them instead of home economics and woodwork? There are three answers to that. First, we need woodworkers.

Second, people have always been suspicious of rhetoric in general and the figures in particular. If somebody learns how to phrase things beautifully, they might be able to persuade you of something that isn't true. Stern people dislike rhetoric, and unfortunately it's usually stern people who are in charge: solemn fools who believe that truth is more important than beauty.

Third, the Romantic Movement came along at the end of the eighteenth century. The Romantics liked to believe that you could learn everything worth learning by gazing at a babbling mountain brook, or running barefoot through the fields, or contemplating a Grecian urn. They wanted to be natural, and the figures of rhetoric are not natural. They are formulas, formulas that you can learn from a book.

So what with the dislike of beauty and books, the figures of rhetoric were largely forgotten. But that doesn't mean that they ceased to be used. You see, when the Ancient Greeks were going around collecting their formulas, they weren't plucking them out of thin air or growing them in a test tube. All that the Greeks were doing was noting down the best and most memorable phrases they heard, and working out what the structures were, in much the same way that when you or I eat a particularly delicious meal, we might ask for the recipe.

The figures are, to some extent, alive and well. We still use them. It's just that we use them haphazardly. What Shakespeare had beaten into him at school, we might, occasionally, use by accident and without realising it. We just happen to say something beautiful, and don't know how we did it. We are like blindfolded cooks throwing anything into the pot and occasionally, just occasionally, producing a delicious meal.

Shakespeare had a big recipe book and his eyes wide open.

The figures are alive and thriving. The one line from that song or film that you remember and *don't know why you remember* is almost certainly down to one of the figures, one of the flowers of rhetoric growing wild. They account for the songs you sing and the poems you love, although that is hidden from you at school.

English teaching at school is, unfortunately, obsessed with what a poet thought, as though that were of any interest to anyone. Rather than being taught about how a poem is phrased, schoolchildren are asked to write essays on what William Blake thought about the Tiger; despite the fact that William Blake was a nutjob whose opinions, in a civilised society, would be of no interest to anybody apart from his parole officer. A poet is not somebody who has great thoughts. That is the menial duty of the philosopher. A poet is somebody who expresses his thoughts, however commonplace they may be, exquisitely. That is the one and only difference between the poet and everybody else.

So my aim in this book is to explain the figures of rhetoric, devoting one chapter to each. There are a couple of caveats that I should make clear before we begin. First of all, the study of rhetoric did not entirely disappear with the Romantics. There are still scholarly articles written. Unfortunately, almost all of these get tied in knots trying to define their terms. Rhetorical terminology, like anything kicked around for a couple of millennia, is a mess. So an article on syllepsis will start by defining the term, attacking other scholars for defining it differently, appealing to the authority of Quintilian or Susenbrotus, and then conclude without actually having said anything about syllepsis or what it is. I've written more on this subject in the Epilogue, but as I have no particular interest in such lexical squabbles I have simply adopted the rule of Humpty-Dumpty: When I use a rhetorical term, it means just what I choose it to mean – neither more nor less.

Second, some of you may think that I am trying to attack Shakespeare or whichever poet I'm quoting. You may consider this a cruel work of debunking, like the spoilsports who uncurtained the Wizard of Oz. Shakespeare is a god and it is sacrilege to unseal his star-ypointing pyramid. Little could be further from the truth. It doesn't insult the Wright Brothers to explain the principles of aerodynamics, nor Neil Armstrong the spacesuit. Shakespeare was a craftsman, and if you told him that now people studied his attitudes to feminism more than his rhetorical figures he would chuckle.

Shakespeare did not consider himself sacred. He would often just steal content from other people. However, whatever he stole he improved, and he improved it using the formulas, flowers and figures of rhetoric.

Chapter 1

⟶ ∞ ⟵

Alliteration

Let us begin with something we know Shakespeare stole, simply so that we can see what a wonderful thief he was. When Shakespeare decided to write *The Tragedie of Anthonie, and Cleopatra* he of course needed a history book from which to work. The standard work on the subject was Plutarch's *Lives of the Noble Greeks and Romans*, but Plutarch wrote in Greek, and, as Shakespeare's friend Ben Jonson later pointed out, 'thou hadst small Latin and less Greek'.

Despite years at Stratford Grammar School learning pretty much nothing but the classics, Shakespeare could never be bothered with foreign languages. He always used translations.

So he got hold of the standard English translation of Plutarch, which had been written by a chap called Thomas North and published in 1579. We know that this is the version Shakespeare used because you can sometimes see him using the same word that North used, and sometimes pairs of words. But when Shakespeare got to the big speech of the whole play, when he really needed some poetry, when he wanted true greatness, when he wanted to describe the moment that Antony saw Cleopatra on the barge and fell in love with her – he just found the relevant paragraph in North and copied it out almost word for word. *Almost* word for word.

Here's North:

> … she disdained to set forward otherwise but to take her barge in the river Cydnus, the poop whereof was of gold, the sails of purple, and the oars of silver, which kept stroke in rowing after the sound of the music of flutes, howboys, citherns, viols, and such other instruments as they played up in the barge.

And here's Shakespeare:

> The barge she sat in like a burnished throne,
> Burned on the water: the poop was beaten gold;
> Purple the sails and so perfumed that
> The winds were lovesick with them; the oars were silver,
> Which to the tune of flutes kept stroke, and made
> The water which they beat to follow faster,
> As amorous of their strokes.

The thing about this is that it's definitely half stolen. There is no possible way that Shakespeare didn't have North open on his desk when he was writing. But also, Shakespeare made little changes. That means that we can actually watch Shakespeare working. We can peep back 400 years and see the greatest writer who ever lived scribbling away. We can see how he did it, and it's really pretty bloody simple. All he did was add some alliteration.

Nobody knows why we love to hear words that begin with the same letter, but we do and Shakespeare knew it. So he picked the word *barge* and worked from there. Barge begins with a B, so Shakespeare sat back and said to himself: 'The barge she sat in was like a …' And then (though I can't prove this) he said: 'Ba … ba … ba … burnished throne.' He jotted that down and then he decided to do another. 'The barge she sat in like a burnished throne … ba … ba … burned? It burned on the water.' And the poop was gold? Not any more: the poop was beaten gold. That's four Bs in two lines. Enough to be getting on with. Shakespeare could have got carried away and written something like:

> The barge she basked in, like a burnished boat
> Burned by the banks, the back was beaten brass.

But that would just be silly. Of course, Shakespeare did write like that sometimes. There's a bit in *A Midsummer Night's Dream* that goes:

> Whereat, with blade, with bloody blameful blade,
> He bravely broached his boiling bloody breast;

But there he was taking the mickey out of poets who use alliteration but don't know where to stop. No, Shakespeare wasn't going to put any more Bs in, he was working on the Ps. North's original had 'the poop whereof was of gold, the sails of purple'. That's two Ps already, so Shakespeare decided that the sails would be pa … pa … perfumed. Maybe he stopped to wonder how you would perfume a whole sail, or how you might be able to smell them from the river bank (the Cydnus is quite wide). Or maybe he didn't. Accuracy is much less important than alliteration.

From there on in, Shakespeare was coasting. North had 'After the sound' so Shakespeare had 'to the tune'. North had a whole orchestra of instruments – 'flutes, howboys, cithernes, viols' – Shakespeare cut that down to just flutes, because he liked the F. So flutes made the 'Water Which they beat to Follow Faster, As Amorous of their strokes'.

So Shakespeare stole; but he did wonderful things with his plunder. He's like somebody who nicks your old socks and then darns them. Shakespeare simply knew that people are suckers for alliteration and that it's pretty damned easy to make something alliterate (or that it's surprisingly simple to add alliteration).

You can spend all day trying to think of some universal truth to set down on paper, and some poets try that. Shakespeare knew that it's much easier to string together some words beginning with the same letter. It doesn't matter what it's about. It can be the exact depth in the sea to which a chap's corpse has sunk; hardly a matter of universal interest, but if you say, 'Full fathom five thy father lies', you will be considered the greatest poet who ever lived. Express precisely the same thought any other way – e.g. 'your father's corpse is 9.144 metres below sea level' – and you're just a coastguard with some bad news.

Any phrase, so long as it alliterates, is memorable and will be believed even if it's a bunch of nonsense. Curiosity, for example, did not kill the cat. There are no widely reported cases of felines dying from being too inquisitive. In fact, the original proverb was not 'curiosity killed the cat' (which is recorded only from 1921), it was 'care killed the cat'. And even that one was changed. When the proverb was first recorded (in Shakespeare, actually, although he seems to be just referring to a well known bit of folk wisdom), care meant sorrow or unhappiness. But by the twentieth century it was care in the sense of too much kindness – something along the lines of a pet that is overfed and pampered. In a hundred years' time it may be something else that does the pussy-killing, although you can be certain that whatever it is – kindness, consternation or corruption – will begin with a C or K.

Similarly, there was once an old proverb, 'An ynche in a misse is as good as an ell', an ell being an old unit of measurement of 45 inches, and therefore A Lot More. That A Lot More became a mile, and then the inch was dropped because it doesn't begin with an M, and we were left with 'A miss is as good as a mile', which, if you think about it, doesn't really make sense any more. But who needs sense when you have alliteration?

Nobody has ever thrown a baby out with the bathwater, nor is there anything particularly right about rain. Even when something does make a bit of sense, it's usually obvious why the comparison was picked. It takes two to tango, but it takes two to waltz as well. There are whole hogs, but why not pigs? Bright as a button. Cool as a cucumber. Dead as a doornail. In fact, Dickens made this point rather better than I at the opening of *A Christmas Carol*.

Old Marley was as dead as a door-nail.

Mind! I don't mean to say that I know, of my own knowledge, what there is particularly dead about a door-nail. I might have been inclined, myself, to regard a coffin-nail as the deadest piece of ironmongery in the trade. But the wisdom of our ancestors is in the simile; and my unhallowed hands shall not disturb it, or the Country's done for. You will therefore permit me to repeat, emphatically, that Marley was as dead as a door-nail.

Except that Dickens knew full well why it is doornails that are dead. Dickens was a writer, and as a writer, he knew that alliteration is the simplest way to turn a memorable phrase. This was, after all, the guy who had written *Nicholas Nickleby*, *The Pickwick Papers* (full title: *The Posthumous Papers of the Pickwick*

Club) and, indeed, *A Christmas Carol*. He knew which side his bread was buttered, as had those who came before him, like Jane Austen (*Sense and Sensibility*, *Pride and Prejudice*), and those who came after him (*Where's Wally?*).

So popular is alliteration that in the 1960s it actually made a grab for political power. In the 1960s a vast radical youth movement began campaigning to do things for the sole reason that they began with the same letter. Ban the bomb. Burn your bra. Power to the people. For a moment there it seemed as though alliteration would change the world. But then the spirit of idealism faded and those who had manned the barricades went off and got jobs in marketing. They stopped telling people to ban the bomb and started telling them to put a tiger in your tank, chuck out the chintz and use Access – Your Flexible Friend, or perhaps PayPal. And all because the lady loves Milk Tray.

It's enough to get your goat.[1]

Alliteration can be brief and obvious – a short, sharp, shock. Or it can be long and subtle. John Keats once wrote fourteen lines of Fs and Ss, and it was beautiful:

Deep in the shady sadness of a vale
Far sunken from the healthy breath of morn,
Far from the fiery noon, and eve's one star,
Sat gray-hair'd Saturn, quiet as a stone,
Still as the silence round about his lair;
Forest on forest hung about his head
Like cloud on cloud. No stir of air was there,
Not so much life as on a summer's day

---

[1] First recorded 1910 with no explanation at all.

Robs not one light seed from the feather'd grass,
But where the dead leaf fell, there did it rest.
A stream went voiceless by, still deadened more
By reason of his fallen divinity
Spreading a shade: the Naiad 'mid her reeds
Press'd her cold finger closer to her lips.

Whereas, at almost the same time, Thomas De Quincey, famous junkie and prose stylist, got himself all muddled up over this sentence:

At present, after exchanging a few parting words, and a few final or farewell farewells with my faithful female agent ...

So muddled was he that he decided to add a footnote apologising for his paroemion (that's the technical name for excessive alliteration). The footnote went:

Some people are irritated, or even fancy themselves insulted, by overt acts of alliteration, as many people are by puns. On their account, let me say, that, although there are here eight separate f's in less than half a sentence, this is to be held as pure accident. In fact, at one time there were nine f's in the original cast of the sentence, until I, in pity of the affronted people, substituted *female agent* for *female friend.*

'Agent' seems a strange substitution for 'friend'. But he probably had to do it as he couldn't change 'farewell farewells'. It's much too clever to use a word as an adjective and then a noun. In fact, the trick has a name. It's called polyptoton.

Chapter 2

——⚬⚬⚬——

Polyptoton

Poor polyptoton is one of the lesser-known rhetorical tricks. It has no glamour. It isn't taught to schoolchildren. It has a silly name which sounds a bit like polyp, a word for a nasal growth. In fact, it comes from the Greek for 'many cases', but that hardly makes up for it. Even once you've explained that that's because it involves the repeated use of one word as different parts of speech or in different grammatical forms, polyptoton remains incorrigibly unsexy. This is a trifle unfair, especially as one of the best known examples of polyptoton is a song that is sometimes said to be about oral sex.

'Please Please Me'[1] is a classic case of polyptoton. The first *please* is please the interjection, as in 'Please mind the gap'. The second *please* is a verb meaning to give pleasure, as in 'This pleases me'. Same word: two different parts of speech. It's easy, once you ponder it, to see how people could feel that the polyptoton was a little perverse.[2]

Whether the song is actually about matters carnal or emotional is beyond the scope of a book like this. All that we know about John Lennon's motivations for writing it is that he had a specific interest in polyptoton (even if he may not have known the name). When Lennon was a child, his mother used to sing

---

[1] Lennon/McCartney.

[2] Thus at least Robert Christgau, music editor of *The Village Voice*.

him a Bing Crosby song called 'Please'. The lyrics went like this:

> Please,
> Lend your little ear to my pleas
> Lend a ray of cheer to my pleas

And Lennon's explanation of his own lyrics[3] was that in that song 'I was always intrigued by the double use of the word "Please"'. Of course, in those lyrics the second *please* is spelled pleas, but that doesn't matter. It's still polyptoton if the words have a close etymological connection, or are just different parts of the same verb, which means that 'All You Need is Love'[4] is pretty much polyptoton beginning to end:

> Nothing you can do that can't be done
> Nothing you can sing that can't be sung

Et cetera et cetera. Of course, John Lennon didn't invent polyptoton. Shakespeare used it all the time. Some of his most famous lines go:

> Let me not to the marriage of true minds
> Admit impediments. Love is not love
> Which alters when it alteration finds,
> Or bends with the remover to remove.

Alters the verb, *alteration* the noun. *Remover* the noun, *remove* the verb. ('Love is not love' is merely a paradox, and we'll come

---

[3] *Playboy* interview, 1980.

[4] Lennon/McCartney.

to that later.) He used it again in *Macbeth* with:

> Is this a dagger that I see before me,
> The handle towards my hand?

In fact, Shakespeare was so fond of polyptoton that he just repeated himself wholesale. He had a trick and he liked it and he used it again and again. So in *Richard II* Bolingbroke, busy revolting, says 'My gracious uncle', but his uncle, the Duke of York replies:

> Tut, tut!
> Grace me no grace, nor uncle me no uncle:
> I am no traitor's uncle; and that word 'grace'
> In an ungracious mouth is but profane.

Which is three counts of polyptoton and jolly clever. In fact, Shakespeare was so pleased with himself that when he got round to writing *Romeo and Juliet* he (hoping nobody would notice that he's just reusing his old lines) has Juliet's dad tell her:

> Thank me no thankings, nor proud me no prouds.

It was just a trick that Shakespeare had in his bag, and a device like that can be devised anywhere you like. In fact, the most famous use of Shakespeare's little trick wasn't by Shakespeare. This makes sense really. Anybody can write 'Hello me no hellos' or 'How are you old chap me no how are you old chaps'. It is a trick available to everyone and the best example was by a lady called Susanna Centlivre.

Susanna Centlivre had a strange life. She ran away from home, may have cross-dressed, may thus have been the first woman educated at Cambridge University, and was certainly the most successful female writer of the eighteenth century. But the only line of hers that has stood the test of time is from *The Busybody*. A son is arguing with his father about the usual father–son issues of money, marriage, and remarriage. The father says:

> *Sir Francis*: Out of my Doors, you Dog; you pretend to meddle with my Marriage, Sirrah.
> *Charles*: Sir, I obey: But—
> *Sir Francis*: But me no Buts— Be gone, Sir: Dare to ask me for Money agen— Refuse Forty Thousand Pound! Out of my Doors, I say, without Reply.

And poor old Shakespeare probably turned once in his grave and mumbled, 'But! I should have used but.'

Of course, these are the most obvious forms of polyptoton: *but* verb versus *but* viewed as a word itself. It's almost too easy to do, but you're bound to come up with a good line, so never say never. Much more subtle are Shakespeare's 'Speak the speech' or 'The rain it raineth every day', both of which could be shortened to 'Speak' or 'It raineth', but they wouldn't sound as good. The son of God tended to use subtler polyptotons. 'Give us this day our daily bread and forgive us our trespasses as we forgive them that trespass against us' is a pretty neat double.

So just as a little recap, polyptoton is a favourite of Jesus, Shakespeare and John Lennon. With a trio like that one can almost forget the smaller voices: Moses' wife saying 'I have been a stranger in a strange land', or William Blake's 'Piper, pipe that song again'. Polyptoton, even though nobody has ever heard of it, succeeds, and nothing succeeds like success. Polyptoton is the sort of rhetorical trope you use when you're the first man on the moon, unless cruelly messed up by the radio transmission. Neil Armstrong's actual words were (beginning on the ladder of the Lunar Excursion Module): 'I'm going to step off the LEM now.' And then, as his boot touched the moon: 'That's one small step for a man, one giant leap for mankind.'

Except that static on the radio cut in and the 'a' in 'for a man' got cut out. This was problematic as it meant that the phrase became utterly meaningless. Without an indefinite article to specify that the small step is being taken by one particular fellow, *man* is being used as a general noun meaning 'mankind'. So the transmission to earth essentially says: 'That's one small step for mankind, one giant leap for mankind.' Which rather ruins the point, not to mention the polyptoton. Of course, you have a bit of polyptoton left: there's the 'to step off' verb against the 'one small step' noun. But nonetheless, it would have been good to begin our first extraterrestrial jaunt with a good, meaningful double-polyptoton.

I should point out that there is a theory that it wasn't the static's fault, and that Neil Armstrong simply fluffed his own lines, something that you could perhaps forgive him for considering the stressful circumstances. It is hard, polyptonically, to talk the talk when you're also trying to moon-walk the moon-walk.

With the missing 'a' returned, the full phrase is also a great example of antithesis.

Chapter 3

---oᴏᴏ---

Antithesis

Polyptoton was complex. Antithesis is simple. Indeed, the only tricky thing about antithesis is how to punctuate it. Some insist that you should use a colon: others complain that you should use a full stop. But in essence antitheses are simple: first you mention one thing: then you mention another.

Of course there are, occasionally, clever antitheses, antitheses that draw fine distinctions or tell you something that you did not know already. Oscar Wilde was the master of these, with lines like, 'The well-bred contradict other people. The wise contradict themselves.' But we can't all be Oscar Wilde, and it would be interminably dull if we were. The world would degenerate into one permanent epigram.

Wildean antitheses are not too hard. You make a first statement that is relatively obvious, for example, 'If a man is a gentleman he knows quite enough.' The second half begins in an obvious way: 'If he is not a gentleman' … and then takes an odd turn: 'whatever he knows is bad for him.'

So 'Wicked women bother one' looks as though it will be followed by 'Good women console one', but instead it is followed by 'Good women bore one.' Or you have 'Women represent the triumph of matter over mind; men represent the triumph of' … and again the reader expects mind over matter, but instead gets 'mind over morals'. Or 'Journalism is unreadable, and literature is not read', or 'If one plays good music, people don't listen, and if one plays bad music people don't talk.' And so on and so forth. So you start with a simple statement – *Some men invent epigrams* – and then you add unexpected inversion – *others are invented by them.*

But these are all just plays on the basic formula of antithesis: X is Y, and not X is not Y. Wilde did a few of these: 'Fashion is what one wears oneself. What is unfashionable is what other people wear.' This is the soul of antithesis, and this is what makes it so simple. Any statement, however basic, can grow into an antithesis. Why just say that life is sweet, when you can add that death is sour? Why point out that the sun rises in the morning without mentioning that it sets in the evening? Of course, anyone could have worked the second halves out for themselves, but what does that matter? United we stand, divided we fall, even though both statements imply the other.

There is something final and certain about a good antithesis. If you said (as you have all right to do, dear reader) that those who can't write themselves instead instruct other people on how to write, who would remember? But say 'Those who can, do: those who can't, teach' and you sound as though you have sliced the world neatly into two and squeezed it out as an epigram.

The Bible is chock-a-block with such unnecessary but beautiful antitheses. God, whatever his other failings, is a great rhetorician.

To every thing there is a season, and a time to every purpose under the heaven: A time to be born, and a time to die; a time to plant, and a time to pluck up that which is planted; A time to kill, and a time to heal; a time to break down, and a time to build up; A time to weep, and a time to laugh; a time to mourn, and a time to dance; A time to cast away stones, and a time to gather stones together; a time to embrace, and a time to refrain from embracing; A time to get, and a time to lose; a time to keep, and a time to cast away; A time to rend, and a time to sew; a time to keep silence, and a time to speak; A time to love, and a time to hate; a time of war, and a time of peace.

If you stop and think about that little passage, you'll notice that it consists mainly of the bleeding obvious, sprinkled with the thoroughly debatable (is there really a time for rending?). But to approach it like that is unfair, irreligious, and shows no appreciation for the beauties of prose. For though one antithesis is grand, a long list of antitheses is divine, and is technically known as a progressio. It was a favourite of God and Dickens:

It was the best of times, it was the worst of times, it was the age of wisdom, it was the age of foolishness, it was the epoch of belief, it was the epoch of incredulity, it was the season of Light, it was the season of Darkness, it was the spring of hope, it was the winter of despair, we had everything before us, we had nothing before us, we were all going direct to Heaven, we were all going direct the other way ...

Or, if you want a more modern magnificence, there is this achingly beautiful disco song by a young lady called Katy Perry:[1]

---

[1] The song 'Hot N Cold' is credited to Katy Perry, Lukasz Gottwald, Max Martin. I have been unable to establish for certain which latter-day Dickens wrote the progressio.

You're hot then you're cold. You're yes then you're no. You're in then you're out. You're up then you're down.

And so on, which is essentially just a reworking of Ecclesiastes. As T.S. Eliot put it: 'Immature poets imitate. Mature poets steal.' Songwriters love their antitheses and there are a million examples I could have used. Unfortunately I noticed that the lyrics 'You say potato and I say potato. You say tomato and I say tomato' don't work that well when they're written down.

However, for some reason the great subject of antithesis seems to be marriage. If I were a philosophical kind of chap I would probably say something about how marriage itself is an antithesis, a union of opposites into a pleasing whole, that man and woman is the ultimate antithesis (and perhaps love and marriage). As I am not a philosophical chap, I shall merely observe that 'Marriage has many pains, but celibacy has no pleasures' (Samuel Johnson), 'Kissing don't last, cookery do' (George Meredith), and 'For better for worse, for richer for poorer, in sickness and in health' … except that, really, that's an example of merism.

Chapter 4

———— ✦ ————

Merism

Merism, ladies and gentlemen, often looks like antithesis, but it's different. Merism is when you don't say what you're talking about, and instead name all of its parts. *Ladies and gentlemen*, for example, is a merism for *people*, because all people are either ladies or gentlemen. The beauty of merism is that it's absolutely unnecessary. It's words for words' sake: a gushing torrent of invention filled with noun and noun and signifying nothing. Why a rhetorical figure that gabs on and on for no good reason should be central to the rite of marriage is beyond me.

> Then shall they give their troth to each other in this manner. The Minister, receiving the Woman at her father's or friend's hands, shall cause the Man with his right hand to take the Woman by her right hand, and to say after him as followeth.
>
> I *N.* take thee *N.* to be my wedded Wife, to have and to hold from this day forward, for better for worse, for richer for poorer, in sickness and in health, to love and to cherish, till death us do part, according to God's holy ordinance; and thereto I plight thee my troth.

You're either better or you're worse, you're either richer or you're poorer, you're either sick or you're healthy. There are no other options. If you need some words there you could say 'in any circumstances'. But really, you don't need to say anything at all.

'Till death us do part' kind of has it sewn up. Anyway, it's all terribly appropriate, as choosing to have two things form a single totality is exactly what marriage is. Even 'loving and cherishing' is a modern replacement for an ancient merism. In the medieval marriage service 'sickness and health' were followed by: 'to be bonny and buxom, in bed and at board, till death do us part.'

Now, this seems to our modern eyes to be a strange sort of promise. How could a wife guarantee that she would be buxom? Were thin women unable to marry in church? However, the word *buxom* has changed in meaning over the years. The first citation in the *Oxford English Dictionary* comes from the twelfth century and is defined as: 'Obedient; pliant; compliant, tractable.' The sense then changed to happy, then to healthy, and thence to plump.

Meanwhile *bonny* comes from the French *bon* and the Latin *bonus*, both of which mean *good*. So a bonny and buxom wife was a good and obedient one. The phrasing was, I assume, deemed to be unreasonably optimistic.

Merism is also the most important feature in gay divorce, or, to be typographically precise about it, in *Gay Divorce*, the 1932 musical by Cole Porter. The hit song from that musical was an exercise in merisms, starting with one of the most common in the English language; 'night and day' is a merism for *always*. 'Night and day you are the one'. It then moves on to the heavens: 'Only you beneath the moon or under the sun', which again means all the time (excluding moonless nights). The song even confesses how unnecessary merisms are: 'Whether near to me or far / It's no matter darling where you are' (his emotions at middle distance are, again, unstated).

It would be tempting to construct an argument that merism is always about love, because love brings opposites together. If you wanted to argue this way (and who's to stop you?), you could cite the song 'Bless 'Em All', which unnecessarily enlarges on the *all* being blessed:

Bless 'em all,
Bless 'em all.
The long and the short and the tall,
Bless all those Sergeants and WO1's,
Bless all those Corporals and their bleedin' sons …

It's all rather lovely that thoughts like that could survive the miseries of war. Uplifts the human spirit, it does. The last two lines strike a strangely angry tone, or at least it's strange until you go back to the original lyrics of 1917, where the word *bless* was replaced by *fuck* throughout.[1]

In fact, merism works for love and hate and everything in between. Tennyson wrote up one of the most memorable in *The Charge of the Light Brigade* where the six hundred have:

Cannon to right of them,
Cannon to left of them,
Cannon in front of them …

The *Oxford English Dictionary* contains the word *quaquaversally* meaning *in every direction*. 'Cannon quaquaversally' would have

---

[1] Fred Godfrey explained the composition of the song in a 1941 letter to the *Daily Mirror*: 'I wrote "Bless 'Em All" while serving in the old R.N.A.S. in France in 1916. And, furthermore, it wasn't "Bless".'

saved time, but wouldn't have been nearly as poetic, and almost everything in Tennyson's most famous poem is there only for the sake of rhetoric. He even pointed out to the editor of the magazine that first published the poem that the charge of the Light Brigade had involved seven hundred men, not six, but 'Six is much better than seven hundred (as I think) metrically so keep it.'

But the true and natural home of merism is in legal documents. Lawyers are like Cole Porter and Alfred Lord Tennyson with a blender. A lawyer, for a reason or reasons known only to him or herself, cannot see a whole without dividing it into its parts and enumerating them in immense detail. This may be something to do with the billing system.

As we've dealt with marriage and divorce, the merism of modern love can be completed with a restraining order. These mirror marriage's merisms with lines like: 'The defendant is prohibited from communicating with the plaintiff, either personally or through other persons, by telephone, writing or any other means.' The second half of that sentence is either utterly redundant, or a challenge. Perhaps there is a way through, perhaps there's a loophole. After all, Cole Porter said that he loved her night and day, but what did he do at twilight? The marriage service promises fidelity in sickness and in health, but might a mild cold bring on a furious bout of adultery? 'Ladies and gentlemen' gets one into all sorts of trouble with those people of no specific gender, although to be fair such ambiguous creatures usually count as both.

The lawyer's lucky phrase is 'including but not limited to', which gets you out of the utterly unnecessary trouble that the utterly unnecessary merism got you into in the first place.

Unfortunately, it's hard to slip that weaselish phrase into the lyrics of 'Night and Day', as they wouldn't scan any more. They might also give a rather bureaucratic feel to a wedding.

Merism searches for wholes, and leaves holes. Thus the most awkward and derided poetic figure is the extended merism, the dismemberment of the loved one: the blazon.

Chapter 5

———∞———

The Blazon (A Merism Too Far)

> Then in the blazon of sweet beauty's best
> Of hand, of foot, of lip, of eye, of brow …

When healthy people fall in love, they buy a bunch of flowers or an engagement ring and go and Do Something About It. When poets fall in love, they make a list of their loved one's body parts and attach similes to them. Your lips are like cherries, your hair is like gold, and your eyes are like traffic lights that make my heart stop and go. These lists are almost universally awkward. Even the Bible starts to sound like the ravings of a lunatic.

> Behold, thou art fair, my love; behold, thou art fair; thou hast doves' eyes within thy locks: thy hair is as a flock of goats, that appear from mount Gilead. Thy teeth are like a flock of sheep that are even shorn, which came up from the washing; whereof every one bear twins, and none is barren among them. Thy lips are like a thread of scarlet, and thy speech is comely: thy temples are like a piece of a pomegranate within thy locks. Thy neck is like the tower of David builded for an armoury, whereon there hang a thousand bucklers, all shields of mighty men. Thy two breasts are like two young roes that are twins, which feed among the lilies.

I suppose that goats had a better reputation back then. And sheep. But nobody's forehead looks like a pomegranate; if it does, they should be rushed to a dermatologist. However, it's not just the choice of similes that makes these lists odd, it's that there are similes at all. If I were to ask you to draw a picture based on that blazon, you'd end up with someone (or something) rather peculiar, and not in the slightest bit attractive.

This hasn't stopped poets going on like surrealist anatomy textbooks for millennia. Take out your sketch-pad again and attempt this lady from Thomas Watson's *Hekatompathia* (1582):

Hark you that list to hear what saint I serve:
Her yellow locks exceed the beaten gold;
Her sparkling eyes in heav'n a place deserve;
Her forehead high and fair of comely mold;
    Her words are music all of silver sound;
    Her wit so sharp as like can scarce be found;
Each eyebrow hangs like Iris in the skies;
Her Eagle's nose is straight of stately frame;
On either cheek a Rose and Lily lies;
Her breath is sweet perfume, or holy flame;
    Her lips more red than any Coral stone;
    Her neck more white than aged Swans that moan;
Her breast transparent is, like Crystal rock;
Her fingers long, fit for Apollo's Lute;
Her slipper such as Momus dare not mock;
Her virtues all so great as make me mute:
    What other parts she hath I need not say,
    Whose face alone is cause of my decay.

One can pretty much guarantee that Mr Watson never got to see her other parts after that effort, and if that poem seems somehow familiar, it's probably because of Shakespeare's parody:

> My mistress' eyes are nothing like the sun
> Coral is far more red than her lips' red;
> If snow be white, why then her breasts are dun;
> If hairs be wires, black wires grow on her head.
> I have seen roses damask'd, red and white,
> But no such roses see I in her cheeks;
> And in some perfumes is there more delight
> Than in the breath that from my mistress reeks.
> I love to hear her speak, yet well I know
> That music hath a far more pleasing sound;
> I grant I never saw a goddess go;
> My mistress, when she walks, treads on the ground:
> And yet, by heaven, I think my love as rare
> As any she belied with false compare.

Mind you, I can't imagine that Shakespeare's mistress was terribly charmed with that description either. There's something basically and horribly wrong with cutting somebody up and replacing them with a bunch of inanimate objects; doing it symbolically in verse is also slightly disturbing. If you took them at all seriously you'd be talking about something that was no longer recognisable as a living human being, which is where Shakespeare ended up. The final and finest blazon is an epitaph for a drowned man:

Full fathom five thy father lies;
Of his bones are coral made;
Those are pearls that were his eyes;
Nothing of him that doth fade,
But doth suffer a sea-change
Into something rich and strange.

The idea that an oyster has eaten and then excreted your eyeballs
is about as romantic as the blazon gets, yet it continues. People
are never people, they're scrapbooks, from Petrarch's Laura to
Dolly Parton's Jolene. Jolene is composed of ivory, emeralds and
unseasonable rain (skin, eyes and voice). But her smile is like a
breath of spring, which is an example of synaesthesia.

Chapter 6

———— ⊗⊗⊗ ————

Synaesthesia

She smelled the way the Taj Mahal looks by moonlight.
The Little Sister by Raymond Chandler

Synaesthesia is either a mental condition whereby colours are perceived as smells, smells as sounds, sounds as tastes etc., or it is a rhetorical device whereby one sense is described in terms of another. If colours are harmonious or a voice is silky, that is synaesthesia (or some other spelling).

It is a common enough device, except that there seem to be rules or norms governing which senses can be coupled. Sight and sound are interchangeable. Quite aside from John Lennon's request to George Martin that the orchestration of 'Strawberry Fields' should be 'orange', colours can be loud or discordant while melodies can be bright and rumblings dark. *Tone* is even an ambiguous word that can be applied to either sense. (I omit colours that are purely symbolic: blues music is no more blue than blue movies are.)

Touch can be applied to sound – a gravelly voice – and to sight – the warm colours of a painting. But rarely is the favour returned; indeed, I can't think of a single example.

Taste gives you a couple of terms of approbation – delicious and tasty – and of deprecation – bland or disgusting. But again it receives no thanks from its fellow senses.

And smell. Smell sits apart on his own, blowing his nose. *Odious*, before you ask, means hateful and has nothing to do with *odour*. Rank and pungent have, over the centuries, been sent as emissaries to the other senses, but that is all and it is possible to forget that those words were ever native to a nostril. And smells are never described as being like anything else at all.

And that is why the Raymond Chandler line is so striking. Though the sense is quite discernible, the expression of it pulls you up short. The phrase is memorable in a way that it would never have been if it were, 'She sounded the way the Taj Mahal looks by moonlight'.

Synaesthesias of smell are jarring and effective, and are probably an easy shortcut to a memorable line. However, caution, dear reader, should be observed. You may not want your line to be remembered. Many critics have been wrong, some amazingly so, but few will be remembered as Eduard Hanslick is; he wrote of Tchaikovsky's First Violin Concerto that it showed there could be 'music that stinks to the ear'.

Synaesthesia reaches its purest form, though, when, rather than shuffling the senses, a sense is given to something completely abstract. Victory does not look like anything visible or sound like anything audible or taste like anything edible, but it has a smell, a smell memorably described in *Apocalypse Now*.

> I love the smell of napalm in the morning. You know, one time we had a hill bombed, for twelve hours. [...] The smell, you know that gasoline smell, the whole hill. Smelled like ... victory. Someday this war's gonna end ...

Which is an example of aposiopesis.

Chapter 7

Aposiopesis

Aposiopesis is when …
Aposiopesis is …
Aposiopesis …

All of the above is technically true, as aposiopesis is signalled in English punctuation by three dots. Like … like this … Aposiopesis is Greek for *becoming silent* and it's the reason that we do not live in Paradise.

There were two important trees in the Garden of Eden: the Tree of Knowledge and the Tree of Life. We chose the wrong one. The fruit of the Tree of Life would have given us immortality. The fruit of the Tree of Knowledge informed us that we were nude, which, as knowledge goes, is pretty low down the list of amazing facts. If my greatest grandmother had picked differently I would be able to expose myself for eternity without anybody realising. If only …

But to return to aposiopesis. God didn't want anybody to notice they were naked. Why God didn't want this is unexplained, but I have my theories … Once the game was up, He cursed Adam, Eve and the talking snake, and then He said:

And now, lest he put forth his hand, and take also of the tree of life, and eat, and live for ever … Therefore the Lord God sent him forth from the garden of Eden, to till the ground from whence he was taken.

You will notice that God did not finish His sentence. Mankind left paradise without a main verb. Theologically, this presents some odd questions. First, God appears to have been talking to Himself. Second, why did he not finish His sentence? He must have been capable of it. He's omnipotent and does not suffer from sore throats and forgetfulness. This does not fit either of the three usual reasons for aposiopesis: that you can't go on, that you don't need to go on, or that you want to leave the audience hanging.

The simplest reason for aposiopesis is death. In fact, the Tree of Life would have robbed us of all those whodunit scenes where a chap stumbles in with a knife between his shoulder blades and just enough breath in his body to tell the detective 'It was … It was …' before giving up the ghost and returning to the ground from whence he came, usually with his finger pointing towards a Vital Clue. Shakespeare does it a little better in *Henry IV Part 1* with the death of Henry Percy. Percy has just enough breath in his body for a good bit of anadiplosis (q.v.) and a final aposiopesis:

> But thought's the slave of life, and life time's fool;
> And time, that takes survey of all the world,
> Must have a stop. O, I could prophesy,
> But that the earthy and cold hand of death
> Lies on my tongue: no, Percy, thou art dust
> And food for …

And just in case the audience was wondering what creature would have had gastronomic designs on the dying hero, Prince Hal explains, 'For worms, brave Percy'. It's rude to finish other people's sentences, unless you killed them first.

Sometimes, though, aposiopesis is because you simply don't know what to say. This can leave you looking rather foolish, like a parent trying to get children to do something but not being able to think, offhand, of an appropriate threat. Thus poor King Lear with his naughty daughters:

> No, you unnatural hags,
> I will have such revenges on you both,
> That all the world shall … I will do such things …
> What they are, yet I know not: but they shall be
> The terrors of the earth.

Which is a much more verbose version of the common or garden aposiopesis: 'Tidy your room, or else …' Sometimes an aposiopesis can make a threat more impressive, as the threatee will write all his or her worst fears on the dotted line. So Samuel Beckett in the novel *Murphy* has:

> 'Have fire in this garret before night or—'
> He stopped because he could not go on. It was an aposiopesis of the purest kind. Ticklepenny supplied the missing consequences in various versions, each one more painful than any that Murphy could have specified, terrifying taken all together.

But King Lear is just too tired and emotional to work out exactly what he plans to do. He *can't* finish his sentence. This is, of course, an easy and effective thing to fake. If you're too over-come to even finish your sentence then you must be sincere, you must really mean what you're not saying, you must … I'm sorry. I cannot type. My fingers are crying.

In *Julius Caesar*, Antony, while doing a very calculated job of stirring up the people of Rome to rebellion, pretends that he's too sad to speak:

> You all did love him once, not without cause:
> What cause withholds you then, to mourn for him?
> O judgment! thou art fled to brutish beasts,
> And men have lost their reason. Bear with me;
> My heart is in the coffin there with Caesar,
> And I must pause till it come back to me.

But God, as we have said, should have more self-control than that.[1] The natural conclusion is that God is using the other form of aposiopesis, the form where the second half of the sentence is so bleeding obvious that it's not even worth saying.

> When in Rome …
> Speak of the Devil …
> Out of the mouths of babes …

Such lines are so familiar that the writer need shed no ink in their conclusion. When in Rome, do as the Romans do. But as God was engaged in the first recorded conversation, he probably

---

[1] Raising the theological question of whether an omnipotent being can control himself.

wasn't using this sort of aposiopesis at all. Rome wasn't built, there were as yet no babes, and the Devil, in snake form, had already appeared. No, God seems to have used aposiopesis for the sheer joy of it. He wanted to be the first being to break off mid ...

Perhaps God's silence is as mysterious as that of the advertisers, who never tell you what would happen 'If only everything in life was as reliable as a Volkswagen'. God moves in a mysterious way, his wonders to perform, which is an example of hyperbaton.

Chapter 8

———∞∞∞———

Hyperbaton

Hyperbaton is when you put words in an odd order, which is very, very difficult to do in English. Given that almost everything else in the English language is slapdash, happy-go-lucky, care-may-the-Devil, word order is surprisingly strict. John Ronald Reuel Tolkien wrote his first story aged seven. It was about a 'green great dragon'. He showed it to his mother who told him that you absolutely couldn't have a green great dragon, and that it had to be a great green one instead. Tolkien was so disheartened that he never wrote another story for years.

The reason for Tolkien's mistake, since you ask, is that adjectives in English absolutely have to be in this order: opinion-size-age-shape-colour-origin-material-purpose Noun. So you can have a lovely little old rectangular green French silver whittling knife. But if you mess with that word order in the slightest you'll sound like a maniac. It's an odd thing that every English speaker uses that list, but almost none of us could write it out. And as size comes before colour, green great dragons can't exist.

There are other rules that everybody obeys without noticing. Have you ever heard that patter-pitter of tiny feet? Or the dong-ding of a bell? Or hop-hip music? That's because, when you repeat a word with a different vowel, the order is always I A O. Bish bash bosh. So politicians may flip-flop, but they can never flop-flip. It's tit-for-tat, never tat-for-tit.[1] This is called *ablaut* reduplication, and if you do things any other way, they sound very, very odd indeed.

The importance of English word order is also the reason that the idea that you can't end a sentence with a preposition is utter hogwash. In fact, it would be utter hogwash anyway, and anyone who claims that you can't end a sentence with *up*, should be told up to shut. It is, as Shakespeare put it, such stuff as dreams are made on, but it's one of those silly English beliefs that flesh is heir to.

Still, it's a favourite line of English teachers who Haven't Thought It Through. The rule is often unfairly blamed on a chap called Robert Lowth who wrote a book called *A Short Introduction to English Grammar* (1762). But all that book actually says is this:

PREPOSITIONS have Government of Cases; and in English they always require the Objective Case after them: as, '*with him, from her, to me.*'

The Preposition is often separated from the Relative which it governs and joined to the Verb at the end of the Sentence, or of some member of it: as, 'Horace is an author, *whom* I am much delighted *with.*' 'The world is too well bred to shock authors with a truth, *which* generally their booksellers are the first that inform them *of.*' This is an Idiom which our language is strongly inclined to; it prevails in common conversation, and suits very well with the familiar style in writing; but the placing of the Preposition before the Relative is more graceful as well as more perspicuous; and agrees much better with the solemn and elevated Style ... But in English the Preposition is more

---

[1] Except in extremely cheap brothels.

frequently placed after the Verb, and separate from it like an Adverb; in which Situation it is no less apt to affect the Sense of it, and to give it a new Meaning; and may still be considered as belonging to the Verb, and a part of it. As *to cast* is to throw; but *to cast up*, or to compute, an account, is quite a different thing: thus *to fall on*, *to bear out*, *to give over* &c. So that the Meaning of the Verb, and the Propriety of the Phrase, depend upon the Preposition subjoined.

Any phrasal verb in the imperative has to end with a preposition. Otherwise, you'd shout 'Out look! Down get! On we are being fired!' Referees would say 'On play'. Off would take planes. And nobody would be allowed to sleep in.

In fact, the most famous example of hyperbaton in English comes from a civil servant twisting a sentence round to get the preposition away from the end. Nobody actually knows what the sentence was. All that history records is that Winston Churchill underlined it and wrote in the margin: 'This is the kind of English up with which I will not put.'

Hyperbaton is a slap in the face to any English speaker, and when it works it goes straight into the language. In 1642 a chap called Richard Lovelace was stuck in prison, pining for his girlfriend. He wrote her a poem about how he wasn't really in prison, and proved it with metaphor. The last verse began:

Stone walls do not a prison make,
Nor iron bars a cage …

Which is a) hyperbaton because *make* should come between *not* and *a*, b) technically untrue and c) quoted so much that it has become part of the language. And not just that exact line, any variant can be used: *adjective noun* does not a *noun* make. So, 333 years after the original was written, in the American television series *Moonlighting*,[2] the Cybill Shepherd character says: 'Well, let me remind you, Mr Addison, that one case does not a detective make.' To which the Bruce Willis character replies: 'Well, let me remind you, Ms Hayes, that I hate it when you talk backwards.'

And all because Mr Lovelace had to make his poem scan.

Uneasy lies the head that wears the crown is one hell of a lot more memorable than *The head that wears the crown lies uneasily*. But when hyperbaton doesn't work it can just be odd. Milton had a bit of a weakness for hyperbaton. Sometimes it worked, as in *pastures new*, and sometimes it really didn't, as in this bit from *Paradise Lost*:

Him who disobeys, me disobeys.

It's a sentence that's liable to make you cock your head on one side and frown. A translation into something approaching English would be 'Whoever disobeys him, disobeys me', but that takes some working out. To be fair to Milton, it would make perfect sense in Latin, but Latin died a long, long time ago. Mind you, the only being who's ever really been able to carry off consistent hyperbaton in English lived a long, long time ago in a galaxy far, far away. In Dagobah, to be precise. And even Yoda dropped hyperbaton when he could get in a good bit of anadiplosis.

---

[2] Created by Glenn Gordon Caron.

Chapter 9

——◦◦◦——

Anadiplosis

Yoda[1] is known for wrong his word order getting, but his most quoted line, from *Star Wars, Episode 1: The Phantom Menace*, uses a different figure entirely. Yoda announces that fear leads to anger. He then takes the last word of that sentence and repeats it as the first word of the next: anger leads to hatred. He then takes the last word of that sentence and repeats it as the first word of the next: hatred leads to suffering. This is a case of anadiplosis. It links him directly to a previous spiritual teacher: St Paul.

> We glory in tribulations also, knowing that tribulation worketh patience, and patience, experience, and experience, hope, and hope maketh man not ashamed.

It is the anadiplosis, the repetition of the last word of one clause as the first word of the next, that gives both lines their power, whether they're written by a saint or uttered by a small green alien.

The content doesn't matter much. In fact, anadiplosis doesn't care what you say and will give its gravitas to a diametrically opposed opinion. Yoda seems to think suffering a bad thing, but there's another semi-fictional American character called Jesse Jackson who observed that:

---

[1] Yoda is a fictional character created by George Lucas.

Suffering breeds character; character breeds faith; in the end faith will not disappoint.

And anyway, Yoda's lines look similar to those of Richard II (as set down by one William Shakespeare):

The love of wicked men converts to fear;
That fear to hate, and hate turns one or both
To worthy danger and deserved death

So between Yoda, Jesse Jackson and Shakespeare we may have a change in philosophy. This isn't necessarily a bad thing. Malcolm X observed that:

Once you change your philosophy, you change your thought pattern. Once you change your thought pattern, you change your attitude. Once you change your attitude, it changes your behavior pattern and then you go on into some action.

And action, in my experience, ends in tiredness and the need for a drink. Drink leads to drunkenness. Drunkenness leads to a hangover. Hangovers cause suffering. Suffering leads to …

But anyway, this chain has gone on for long enough and one cannot be quite sure where it starts and ends, only that it sounds lovely because of anadiplosis. Anadiplosis gives the illusion of logic. Like a conquering general it arrives at a word, plants a flag there, and then moves on. By doubling down it makes everything seem strong, structured and certain.

Of course, that doesn't mean that things *are* strong, structured and certain. There's a logical fallacy called the *quaternio terminorum*, or fallacy of the four terms, that goes something like this:

> A ham sandwich is better than nothing. Nothing is better than eternal happiness. So eternal happiness is beaten by a ham sandwich.

The trick there is that the specific meaning of *nothing* has been changed from 'lack of food' to 'impossibility'. Yoda could have said that fear leads to running away, and running away leads to safety. If the line had simply been 'Fear leads to anger, which leads to hate, which leads to suffering' it wouldn't have sounded half as good, or half as convincing. But with the doubling of anadiplosis, it feels like an inevitable progress.

Of course, anadiplosis doesn't have to be used for logic. It can simply add a harmony, in the same way that a repeated musical phrase binds two sections together. So Milton, mourning his dead friend in *Lycidas*, wrote:

> For Lycidas is dead, dead ere his prime;

And later:

> But O the heavy change now thou art gone,
> Now thou art gone and never must return.

Anadiplosis gives the glue and connection to the Lennon and McCartney song 'Here, There and Everywhere':

> To lead a better life, I need my love to be here.
>
> Here, making each day of the year,

Changing my life with the wave of her hand,
Nobody can deny that there's something there.

There, running my hands through her hair,
Both of us thinking how good it can be,
Someone is speaking but she doesn't know he's there.

There's simply a satisfaction, half logical and half beautiful, in seeing the same word ending one phrase and coming back to life at the start of the next. It is progression. Progression is a story. A story leads to a climax, just as here leads there and there leads everywhere. As the Emperor Commodus (didn't actually) put it when chatting to the (utterly fictional) Maximus Decimus Meridius Russellus Crowus in the film *Gladiator*:

The general who became a slave. The slave who became a gladiator. The gladiator who defied an emperor. Striking story.

And it is, but only when anadiplosis is on hand. *The general who became a slave who became a gladiator who defied an emperor* would sound like a rather incoherent nursery rhyme. But perhaps the greatest anadiplosis is not biblical or Shakespearian, it's simply a description of a dismal dinner, and nobody knows who wrote it:

If the soup had been as warm as the wine, and the wine as old as the fish, and the fish as young as the maid, and the maid as willing as the hostess, it would have been a very good meal.

Which is an example of a periodic sentence.

Chapter 10

Periodic Sentences

The little dot at the end of a sentence is either called a full stop or, if you're of the American persuasion, a period. In fact, Americans rather like saying the word *period* aloud in order to add emphasis, as in, 'You can't do that, period!', or, 'We'll wait a certain amount of time, period!' This all goes back to the notion of a period as a complete cycle of time, and thus a complete, or periodic, sentence.

The period is one of the most complicated and convoluted concepts of classical rhetoric. Nobody in the ancient world could quite decide what it meant, but they were united in the belief that it was terribly, terribly important. Fortunately, in English we tend to take a much more limited view and the periodic sentence is simply a very big sentence that is not complete until the end.

Now you might think that no sentence is complete until the end, but you'd be wrong. That last sentence *could* have finished at the comma, the *but you'd be wrong* was not grammatically necessary. In fact, if you'd got bored halfway through, you could have put this book down and gone off to make a cup of tea with no syntactic shadow hanging over you. The same cannot be said of Rudyard Kipling's poem 'If'.

'If' is one long, 294-word sentence, 273 of which are conditional clauses. If you can keep your head, trust yourself, dream, think etc., then you can finally get to the main verb on the

31st line, and then 'Yours is the Earth and everything that's in it / And – which is more – you'll be a Man, my son!'

The trick of the periodic sentence is that, until you've got to the end, until you've found that clause or verb that completes the syntax, until you've finally got to the period of the period, you can't stop. Kipling forces you along to the climax. Read the first line of 'If' and you have to read on until line 31 before you're grammatically satisfied. And by that time you might as well read line 32, just so you can say you have.

Shakespeare used the same trick, but usually by piling nouns one on top of the other. In *The Tempest* Prospero says:

> And, like the baseless fabric of this vision,
> The cloud-capp'd towers, the gorgeous palaces,
> The solemn temples, the great globe itself,
> Yea, all which it inherit, shall dissolve ...

He knew the reader can't stop until they get to that main verb. The *Tempest* example is actually remarkably restrained for Shakespeare. In John of Gaunt's death scene in *Richard II*, the old man is meant to be so ill he can barely speak. One wonders, therefore, how he managed to take a breath deep enough for this periodic parade:

> This royal throne of kings, this scepter'd isle,
> This earth of majesty, this seat of Mars,
> This other Eden, demi-paradise,
> This fortress built by Nature for herself
> Against infection and the hand of war,
> This happy breed of men, this little world,

This precious stone set in the silver sea,
Which serves it in the office of a wall,
Or as a moat defensive to a house,
Against the envy of less happier lands,
This blessed plot, this earth, this realm, this England,
This nurse, this teeming womb of royal kings,
Fear'd by their breed and famous by their birth,
Renowned for their deeds as far from home,
For Christian service and true chivalry,
As is the sepulchre in stubborn Jewry,
Of the world's ransom, blessed Mary's Son,
This land of such dear souls, this dear dear land,
Dear for her reputation through the world,
Is now leased out, I die pronouncing it,
Like to a tenement or pelting farm …

The substance of that sentence is 'England is now leased out'. Everything else is, from the point of view of content, irrelevant. But 'England is now leased out' is much too tedious, and Shakespeare knew that content was not nearly as important as form. If you want to know what actually happened to Richard II, read a history book. Shakespeare is in it for the periods.

So long as you remember not to blurt out your main verb too early, so long as you begin clause after clause with *when* or *if* or *though* or *while* or *so long*, so long as you have very large lungs that can keep you going through fourteen apposite clauses for England (despite the fact that you're on your death bed), so long as you don't mind being a tad artificial, periodic sentences are a doddle.

In the song 'Every Breath You Take', even in the midst of a jealous rage, Sting still maintained the self-control to save his main verb for the end of the verse:

> Every breath you take,
> Every move you make,
> Every bond you break,
> Every step you take,
> I'll be watching you.[1]

Likewise, in the Four Tops' 'Reach Out I'll Be There' you have a long series of temporal clauses introduced by the word 'when' before you get your reassurance.

However, you don't need to keep using exactly the same structures to stop the sentence finishing. Kipling had his conditional clauses, Shakespeare and Sting their nouns, but Milton managed to hold off the first verb of *Paradise Lost* by digging a huge grammatical hole and setting up camp in it. Like this:

> Of man's first disobedience and the fruit
> Of that forbidden tree, whose mortal taste
> Brought death into the world, and all our woe,
> With loss of Eden, till one greater Man
> Restore us, and regain the blissful seat,
> Sing Heav'nly Muse …

Which is an example of hypotaxis.

---

[1] 'Every Breath You Take' (Gordon Sumner).

Chapter 11

— ∞ —

Hypotaxis and Parataxis
(and Polysyndeton and Asyndeton)

Before we get to hypotaxis, we've got to go through parataxis. Parataxis is like this. It's good, plain English. It's one sentence. Then it's another sentence. It's direct. It's farmer's English. You don't want to buy my cattle. They're good cattle. You don't know cattle. I'm going to have a drink. Then I'm going to break your jaw. I'm a paratactic farmer. My cattle are the best in England.

Parataxis is the natural way of speaking English. It's the way English wants to be spoken. English is a basically uninflected language. Everything depends on the word order. It's all subject verb object. The man kicked the dog. The cat sat on the mat. The angels have the phone box. In Latin and German it's different. Words can be moved around, but you still understand the sentence because of the endings. 'Nauta amat puellam' and 'Puellam nauta amat' both mean 'The sailor loves the girl'. English isn't like that. It's paratactic. It's linear. It's one sentence. Then it's another.

They don't have to be sentences, they could be divided by commas, they could be divided by semi-colons; there's a class of people who get very worked up about such things – they're lonely people – they tend to have stains down the fronts of their shirts – they'll tell you that dashes should be used only to subordinate complete sentences. You must forgive them.

But you can get round the punctuation problem by using conjunctions and just keep your sentence going and going for ever and then chuck in a few buts but not too many then a couple of thens so listen carefully to people telling a story and you'll find that usually there are no full stops and it's just conjunctions and they go on and on for ever.

Using lots of conjunctions is called polysyndeton. No conjunctions is called asyndeton.

> And Jesus took bread, and blessed it, and brake it, and gave it to
> his disciples saying 'Take, eat, this is my body'

So St Mark was very fond of polysyndeton and Jesus was more of an asyndeton chap. There's nothing wrong with parataxis. It's good, simple, clean, plain-living, hard-working, up-bright-and-early English. Wham. Bam. Thank you, ma'am. Orwell liked it. Hemingway liked it. Almost no English writer between about 1650 and 1850 liked it.

The alternative, should you, or any writer of English, choose to employ it (and who is to stop you?) is, by use of subordinate clause upon subordinate clause, which itself may be subordinated to those clauses that have gone before or after, to construct a sentence of such labyrinthine grammatical complexity that, like Theseus before you when he searched the dark Minoan mazes for that monstrous monster, half bull and half man, or rather half woman for it had been conceived from, or in, Pasiphae, herself within a Daedalian contraption of perverted intention, you must unravel a ball of grammatical yarn lest you wander for ever, amazed in the maze, searching through dark eternity for a full stop.

That's hypotaxis, and it used to be everywhere. It's hard to say who started it, but the best candidate was a chap called Sir Thomas Browne.

In 1671, King Charles II visited Norwich and decided he'd like to give someone a knighthood. It didn't matter who. Charles just enjoyed knighting people. The trouble was that there weren't many people in Norwich who seemed to need knighting. Somebody suggested the mayor, but the mayor, apparently, was not really knight material. They settled instead on a doctor called Thomas Browne. Thomas Browne was nothing special as a doctor; but he was the first ever English prose writer, and that's got to be worth a good knighting.

Some people (foolish, deranged and sinister people) will tell you that Sir Thomas Browne was not the first English prose writer. They will point out (quite unhelpfully) that people had been writing English prose for nearly a thousand years before Browne was born. They'll tell you all about Aelfric, Bacon and the King James Bible – Shakespeare, they'll point out, sometimes wrote prose. They'll demonstrate, using mere fact, that I'm talking nonsense. But facts obscure the truth, which is that writing prose doesn't make you a prose writer any more than philosophising makes you a philosopher or fooling around makes you a fool. Or to put it another way:

> Many from the ignorance of these Maxims, and an inconsiderate zeal unto Truth, have too rashly charged the troops of error, and remain as Trophies unto the enemies of Truth: A man may be in as just possession of Truth as of a City, and yet be forced to surrender.

You see, up until Browne, people wrote prose for three reasons: 1) They couldn't be bothered to write poetry (Aelfric). 2) They were translating something and had to make it precise (the Bible). 3) They were trying to write in the way that normal people speak (Shakespeare). Sir Thomas Browne was the first person to write prose because he was damn well writing prose. He wasn't translating anything. He wasn't imitating the man on the street, because no man on any street ever spoke sentences like his. Browne's prose was an awful lot more complicated than poetry. He used hypotaxis, with sentences hidden inside sentences like Russian dolls, clauses hidden in clauses, prepositions referring this way and that, until the bemused reader needs a diagram just to find out where the main verb is. Browne adored hypotaxis, and built huge rococo sentences filled with trap-doors and secret passages and little subordinate clauses dancing around. Here he is on the subject of whether the Bible is literally true:

> … thus is man that great and true Amphibium, whose nature is disposed to live not onely like other creatures in divers elements, but in divided and distinguished worlds; for though there bee not one to sense, there are two to reason; the one visible, the other invisible, whereof Moses seemes to have left description, and of the other so obscurely, that some parts thereof are yet in controversie; and truely for the first chapters of Genesis, I must confesse a great deale of obscurity, though Divines have to the power of humane reason endeavoured to make all goe in a literall meaning, yet those allegoricall interpretations are also probable, and perhaps the mysticall method of Moses bred up in the Hieroglyphicall Schooles of the Egyptians.

Browne gave to the English language the glory of the preposterously long sentence: sentences that nobody in their right minds would ever say aloud, sentences that are intricate games, filled with fine flourishes and curious convolutions. Such sentences have a remarkable quality: civilisation.

Hypotaxis is unnatural in English; nobody would ever say a sentence like the one above. You have to think calmly for a long time to come up with a good hypotactic sentence, and so a good hypotactic sentence tells the reader that you have been thinking calmly for long time. An angry drunk might shout paratactically; only a just and gentle mind can be hypotactic.

If someone was furious about a sycophantic lawyer they might say: 'Lawyers are only interested in money. Sure, lawyers pay you compliments. Compliments are free.' But when Charles Dickens said exactly the same thing, he phrased it like this:

> It was a maxim with Mr Brass that the habit of paying compliments kept a man's tongue oiled without any expense; and that, as that useful member ought never to grow rusty or creak in turning on its hinges in the case of a practitioner of the law, in whom it should be always glib and easy, he lost few opportunities of improving himself by the utterance of handsome speeches and eulogistic expressions.

Seventy-three words of hypotactic fun that somehow never seems rude, even though it definitely is. Indeed, if Mr Brass were allowed to read his creator's description of him, he would probably have chuckled. But hypotaxis doesn't just stop you being rude, it stops you being too enthusiastic as well. You can't gush with hypotaxis. If I told you: 'She's beautiful and clever and rich.

She's got a lovely house. She's always friendly. She has all the best things that a person can have. She's 21. Nothing bad ever happens to her', you'd think that I was afflicted with the most tedious variety of love, and you probably wouldn't believe me. But Jane Austen wrote exactly the same thing as the first line of *Emma*:

> Emma Woodhouse, handsome, clever, and rich, with a comfortable home and happy disposition, seemed to unite some of the best blessings of existence; and had lived nearly twenty-one years in the world with very little to distress or vex her.

You can almost see Miss Austen winking at you over a cup of tea.

Absolutely anything sounds civilised and well-thought-out, provided that it's expressed in the most syntactically complicated, hyper-hypotactic manner. And so from 1650 to 1850 everybody sounded civilised and wise. Even pornography had an air of considered calm to it, now lost for ever to the discerning pervert. *Fanny Hill* (1748) is generally thought the greatest mucky novel in English literature. Its content is, of course, much like the content of any dirty story, human nature being what it is, and the human body having only so many viable entrances and exits; but when such coarsely eternal activities are laced into a mad grammarian's fantasy, the result is superb.

> Coming then into my chamber, and seeing me lie alone, with my face turned from the light towards the inside of the bed, he, without more ado, just slipped off his breeches, for the greater ease and enjoyment of the naked touch; and softly turning up

my petticoats and shift behind, opened the prospect of the back avenue to the genial seat of pleasure; where, as I lay at my side length, inclining rather face downward, I appeared full fair, and liable to be entered. Laying himself gently down by me, he invested me behind, and giving me to feel the warmth of his body, as he applied his thighs and belly close to me, and the endeavours of that machine, whose touch has something so exquisitely singular in it, to make its way good into me.

If one attempts to rewrite that in the paratactic style, it loses all its charm and might indeed be considered almost smutty, almost vulgar.

Hypotaxis was what made English prose so terribly, terribly civilised. It still works. Angry letters of complaint, redundancy notices and ransom notes will, if written in careful hypotaxis, sound as reasonable, measured and genial as a good dose of rough Enlightenment pornography.

Yet hypotaxis (along with reason) has been declining for a century or more. Gone are those heady and incomprehensible sentences of Johnson, Dickens and Austen, replaced with the cruel, brutalist parataxes of writers whose aim is to agitate and distress. The long sentence is now a ridiculed rarity, usually hidden away in the Terms and Conditions, its commas and colons, clauses and caveats languishing unread and unloved.

The long sentence did have one last hurrah, though, one farewell bash before it was retired to exhausted obscurity. The last sentence of James Joyce's *Ulysses* is 4,391 words long and has no punctuation at all, not a dash or a semi-colon from its opening to its last words: 'yes I said yes I will Yes.'

Which is an example of diacope.

Chapter 12

⟨∞⟩

Diacope

In 1962 cinema-goers were introduced to a new hero and a new Great Line. They met him for the first time in Le Cercle casino, but they weren't allowed to see his face. Instead, the camera concentrated on a pretty woman in a red dress who is losing at baccarat. She loses and loses and loses until, finally, she says that she needs to borrow another thousand pounds. And now we hear the hero's voice, off camera. He says, rather sarcastically, 'I admire your courage, Miss ...'

'Trench,' the lady replies tetchily. And then, seeing who's asked the question and clearly finding him attractive, she adds her first name: 'Sylvia Trench.'

Then she, clearly miffed, adds: 'I admire your luck, Mr ...'

The camera turns to the mysterious man; and he, still making fun of her and mimicking her rather silly introduction, says: 'Bond. James Bond.'[1]

It's a tit-for-tat flirtation. They each imitate the other's sentences, until inevitably she goes back to Bond's flat, undresses and plays golf. It wasn't meant to be a great line. Nonetheless, the American Film Institute rates it as the 22nd greatest line in all cinema (how they can be so precise, I don't precisely know). Another poll had it as the best-loved one-liner in the history of

---

[1] *Dr No* (1962), written by Richard Maibaum, Johanna Harwood, Berkely Mather from the novel by Ian Fleming.

film. This is, if you think about it, peculiar. The content of the line, for what it's worth is ... well ... that he's called James Bond. And James Bond is a boring, boring name. It was deliberately chosen to be tedious. Ian Fleming explained:

> I wanted the simplest, dullest, plainest-sounding name I could find, James Bond was much better than something more interesting, like 'Peregrine Carruthers.' Exotic things would happen to and around him, but he would be a neutral figure – an anonymous, blunt instrument wielded by a government department.[2]

So just to recap, one of the greatest lines in the history of cinema is a man saying a name deliberately designed to be dull. The only possible explanation for the line's popularity is the way it is phrased. Would the line have been remembered if he had said 'My name is Mr James Bond', or 'Bond, first name James', or 'Bond, but you can call me James', or 'James Bond'?

Wording, pure wording.

Diacope (pronounced die-ACK-oh-pee) is a verbal sandwich: a word or phrase is repeated after a brief interruption. You take two Bonds and stuff James in the middle. Bingo. You have a great line. Or if you like you can take two burns and stuff a baby in the middle, and you've got a political slogan and disco hit: burn, baby, burn ('Disco Inferno').

If you want to write the greatest line in *The Godfather Part II*, all you need is two *It was you*s with a *Fredo, I know* as the stuffing. In fact, you don't even need to use diacope at all. Diacope

---

[2] Interview with the *Manchester Guardian* (1958).

has a life of its own and flits, like a winged monkey, into places it was never meant to be. Every child remembers how, in *The Wizard of Oz*, the Wicked Witch of the West[3] cries: 'Fly, my pretties, fly!'

Except that she doesn't.

In the film the flying monkeys are instructed to 'Fly! Fly! Fly! Fly!' and there is no vocative *my pretties* to be heard. So why does everybody remember it incorrectly? There is plenty of diacope around in the film. There's 'Run, Toto – run!' and 'I'm frightened, Auntie Em – I'm frightened!'[4] And diacope is powerful, so powerful that it somehow spread in our memories and the witch's *my pretties* slid into every repetition.

British Prime Ministers are always having diacope thrust upon them by the popular imagination. There's a well-known story of a journalist asking Harold Macmillan what the biggest problem was for a government. Harold Macmillan replied, 'Events, dear boy, events.' Except that there is no written record of his ever saying this. He did once talk about the 'opposition of events', but that's it. His best known line is probably not even his, but it is diacope.

In 1979, Britain was in a wintry and discontented state. Inflation was running at 10 per cent and everybody, even the rubbish collectors and grave-diggers, was on strike. James Callaghan, the Prime Minister, on the other hand, was at a trade conference in the Caribbean. When he returned, looking decidedly tanned and healthy, journalists at the airport asked him

---

[3] See chapter on alliteration.

[4] Screenplay by Noel Langley, Florence Ryerson and Edgar Allan Woolf, adapted from the novel by L. Frank Baum. All excerpts from *The Wizard of Oz* granted courtesy of Warner Bros. Entertainment Inc. All Rights Reserved, © 1939.

what he was going to do about the mounting chaos. He replied that 'I don't think other people in the world would share the view that there is mounting chaos.' It is the line for which he is remembered, though not in that phrasing. Diacope had again slithered in and the headline in *The Sun* the next day was 'Crisis? What Crisis?'

It's a shame when your most famous line isn't yours. Several dictionaries of quotations have it under his name, but point out that the line is actually by a *Sun* journalist. They're wrong too. *Crisis? What Crisis?* was the title of a Supertramp album released in 1975, and they appear to have got it from *The Day of the Jackal*.

It doesn't matter whether you intended to deploy diacope. It's rather like the story of James Whistler and Oscar Wilde. Whistler had just made a particularly witty witticism and Wilde ruefully commented, 'I wish I'd said that.' Whistler, who liked to imply that all Wilde's best lines were stolen from him, replied, 'You will, Oscar. You will.' You may not mean to diacopise, but you will, dear reader, you will.

Diacope comes in a number of forms. The simplest is the vocative diacope: *Live, baby, live. Yeah, baby, yeah. I am dying, Egypt, dying. Game over, man, game over. Zed's dead, baby, Zed's dead.*[5] All you do is chuck in somebody's name or their title and repeat. The effect is to put a bit of emphasis, a certain finality, on the second word. Somehow it ceases to be a joke or an off-the-cuff remark and becomes a rhadamantine judgement.

---

[5] In case you were wondering, that's INXS, Austin Powers, *Antony and Cleopatra*, *Aliens* and *Pulp Fiction*.

You can even deploy this with phrases (*They told me, Heraclitus, they told me you were dead*), or whole sentences (*Do you remember an inn, Miranda, do you remember an inn?*).

The other main form of diacope is the elaboration, where you chuck in an adjective. *From sea to shining sea. Sunday bloody Sunday. O Captain! My Captain! Human, all too human. From harmony, from heavenly harmony ...* or *Beauty, real beauty, ends where intellectual expression begins.* This form gives you a feeling both of precision (we're not talking about fake beauty) and crescendo (it's not merely a sea, it's a shining sea).

Or you can combine the two. Dr Johnson once met a lady who was very keen on horses. She asked him why, in his dictionary, he had defined *pastern* as the knee of a horse when in fact, as she helpfully explained, it was the portion below the fetlock. Johnson replied: 'Ignorance, Madam. Pure ignorance.'

Finally there's extended diacope. All the previous examples have had the structure ABA. But you can extend that to AABA. When Richard III is dying he shouts, 'A horse! A horse! My kingdom for a horse!' Shakespeare knew a show-stopping line when he wrote one, which is probably why he stole his own formula for Juliet on her balcony asking, 'Romeo, Romeo, wherefore art thou Romeo?'

(While we're on the subject of this line, I'd like to point out that she's not asking *where* Romeo is. *Wherefore* doesn't mean *where*, it means *why*. Juliet is upset because she's fallen in love with a chap without asking his name, and then found out that he's called Romeo and Romeo is the one chap in Verona that she really shouldn't be getting soppy over.)

Since then the trick has been used again, again and once again. Compare these:

'O villain, villain, smiling, damned villain!'
  – Shakespeare, *Hamlet*

'Alone, alone, all all alone'
  – Coleridge, *The Rime of the Ancient Mariner*

'Dead, dead, long dead, / And my heart is a handful of dust.'
  – Tennyson, *Maud*

'Mud! Mud! Glorious mud!'
  – Flanders and Swann, 'The Hippopotamus Song'

Free at last. Free at last. Thank God almighty we are free at last.
  – Martin Luther King's epitaph, taken from an old spiritual

'Love me. Love me. Say that you love me.'
  – Cardigans, 'Lovefool'

But the greatest example of this extended diacope is the immortal line of Julius Caesar in *Carry on Cleo*: 'Infamy! Infamy! They've all got it in for me.'[6]

Diacope, diacope. They all used diacope. It works. Nobody would have cared if Hamlet had asked 'Whether or not to be?', or 'To be or not?', or 'To be or to die?' No. The most famous line in English literature is famous not for the content, but for the wording. *To be or not to be.*

That is the rhetorical question.

---

[6] Actually, this line was first used on the radio series *Take It From Here* and was recycled for *Carry On Cleo*.

Chapter 13

⸎

Rhetorical Questions

What, O what is a rhetorical question? Is it merely a question that requires no answer? No. Is it a question where the answer is too obvious to need stating? Or one where there is no answer? Or just a cold-blooded thing to say to a chap before you pop a cap in his ass?

Most of us, to be frank, don't know. Including me. The Greeks and Romans had a jolly good shot at it, but they certainly didn't use a term as vague and nebulous as 'rhetorical question'. They distinguished between every different sort of rhetorical question. And then they gave them names. They had erotesis, hypophora, epiplexis, anthypophora, antiphora, apocrisis, interrogatio, rogatio, subjectio, ratiocinatio, dianoea, erotema, epitemesis, percontatio, aporia, and pysma. Isn't that a lot? And each term had a slightly different and very specific meaning. Unfortunately they could never agree what those meanings were, and how one differed from the others, and just when they were getting close they declined, fell, and were overrun by barbarians.

Just to give you an idea of how complicated this all is, the same rhetorical question can be completely different depending on where it's asked. Take the question, 'Which party cares about what's best for Britain?' This might be asked by a Labour leader at a rally of Labour supporters and get the answer 'Labour!' Or it might be asked by the Conservative leader at a rally of Conservative supporters and get the answer 'Conservative!'

(Both of these would be anacoenosis.) Or it might be asked by a solemn and reasonable chap on the telly, who would proceed to weigh up the pros and cons (anthypophora), or it might be asked by a confused chap in the tearful privacy of the polling booth (aporia). And then everything gets more confused if you write the question down in a book, because that way the author doesn't know who's answering.

Shall we begin with erotesis? That's the sort of question that really isn't a question at all. 'Shall I compare thee to a summer's day?' asked Shakespeare, and did not wait for a reply. Fun as it may be to imagine him sending the first line of that sonnet off to his beloved and, a couple of days later, getting the answer, 'Go ahead', I don't think that's what happened. The line could just as easily be: 'I shall compare thee to a summer's day. / Thou art more lovely and more temperate …' but it wouldn't sound as good. The same thing pretty much holds for William Blake's poem about the ancient and preposterous belief that Jesus, before starting his ministry, took a gap year in England.

> And did those feet in ancient time
> Walk upon England's mountains green?

Again, we might be tempted to say no. But that would be to miss the point. 'And did those feet' simply sounds better than 'And those feet did'.

This is the purest form of the rhetorical question, where a couple of words have been switched around and a question mark slapped on the end. It's also a form much loved by Australians. When asked in the Antipodes, 'How bright is the sun?', 'How cute is that koala?' or 'How close is that great white shark?', no answer is required. A question is just their upside-down way of making a statement.

Epiplexis is a more specific form of this where a lament or an insult is asked as a question. *What's the point? Why go on? What's a girl to do? How could you? What makes your heart so hard?* When, in the Bible, Job asks: 'Why died I not from the womb? why did I not give up the ghost when I came out of the belly?', it's not a real question. It's epiplexis. Epiplexis is the puzzled grief of 'Why, God? Why?' in *Miss Saigon*; or it is the bemused disdain in the film *Heathers* that prompts the question: 'Did you have a brain tumour for breakfast?'

Though epiplexis doesn't have a real answer, it does at least have a meaning and a purpose.

Anacoenosis, as we saw above, is the sort of question where a particular audience will answer in a particular way. The Beatles did a song called 'Why Don't We Do It In The Road?'[1] in which fifteen of the eighteen lines are all 'Why don't we do it in the road?'

Now if Paul McCartney were to ask *me* that question, I would have a stack of answers. But we must assume that he's not asking me. He's asking her (whoever she may be). And she can't think of one good reason. Well … maybe one. She may have planned to object that somebody might be watching them. Luckily Mr McCartney has foreseen this objection and the remaining three lines assure her that nobody will be observing (foreseeing and answering a possible objection is a rhetorical device called procatalepsis).

---

[1] Lennon/McCartney.

The thing about anacoenosis is that it makes us realise how much we have in common. We both want to do it in the road. We can both see no serious practical obstacles to doing it in the road. I don't need to tell you how close we are. I can simply ask you questions and we will both know that we have the same answer.[2]

This appeal to shared interests makes politicians particularly fond of anacoenosis. The voter hears the question and automatically gets to the answer that the politician wants. *Who do you trust to run the economy? Would you buy a used car from this man? Why don't we pass a law to stop libidinous Liverpudlians from obstructing traffic?* All these are anacoenosis because all these questions bring out our shared values. Or they're supposed to. *Monty Python*[3] had great fun in *Life of Brian* with the failed anacoenosis of 'What have the Romans ever done for us?' The question is intended as a binding anacoenosis, but unfortunately the audience keep answering until the question has to be restated as: 'All right, apart from the sanitation, medicine, education, wine, public order, irrigation, roads, the fresh water system and public health, what have the Romans ever done for us?' They could have got round this with a good bit of hypophora.

Hypophora is a rhetorical question that is immediately answered aloud, usually by the person who asked. When A Tribe Called Quest recorded the song 'Can I Kick It?', they did not wait for an answer. Instead, the chorus immediately comes back with

---

[2] Although, to be fair, I would add in the uncomfortable nature of asphalt and the danger of passing traffic: two objections missed in McCartney's procatalepsis.
[3] By which I mean Graham Chapman, John Cleese, Terry Gilliam, Eric Idle, Terry Jones and Michael Palin.

the reassuring words *Yes, you can*. No suspicion is allowed to slip into the listener's mind concerning the capabilities of the asker's legs, or the kickability of It (whatever *It* is). They are, at least, a little more succinct than Elizabeth Barrett Browning, who asked, 'How do I love thee? Let me count the ways', and then spent thirteen lines on her reply.

Can you go beyond hypophora? You can. What's that called? Anthypophora. Where is it used? In the nursery rhyme 'Who Killed Cock Robin?' Where else? Well, Winston Churchill rather liked it at times of crisis. When he addressed Parliament on 13 May 1940, with the British army nearly defeated in France and the question of whether to surrender to Germany still being asked, he dodged everything by asking his own questions.

> You ask, what is our policy? I will say it is to wage war, by sea, land, and air, with all our might and all the strength that God can give us; to wage war against a monstrous tyranny, never surpassed in the dark, lamentable catalogue of human crime. That is our policy.
>
> You ask, what is our aim? I can answer in one word: Victory. Victory at all costs, victory in spite of all terror; victory, however long and hard the road may be, for without victory, there is no survival.

Falstaff has a rather more cowardly go at it in *Henry IV Part 1*. He's wondering whether it's worthwhile to die in battle and his reasoning goes thus:

> Well, 'tis no matter; honour pricks [spurs] me on. Yea, but how if honour prick me off when I come on? how then?

Can honour set to a leg? no: or an arm? no: or take away the grief of a wound? no. Honour hath no skill in surgery, then? no. What is honour? a word. What is in that word honour? What is that honour? air. A trim reckoning! Who hath it? he that died o' Wednesday. Doth he feel it? no. Doth he hear it? no. 'Tis insensible, then. Yea, to the dead. But will it not live with the living? no. Why? detraction will not suffer it. Therefore I'll none of it. Honour is a mere scutcheon: and so ends my catechism.

A catechism is a series of questions and answers about religion that you have to memorise. Once you've got the whole thing by rote, a stern and solemn priest will test you on your catechism. He reads out the questions and you recite the responses. Of course, the priest knows the answers already, he just wants to hear you say them.

This is partly because you should really know about the true nature of God and all that sort of stuff. It would be terrible to end up a heretic by mistake. But there's also something immensely powerful, something satisfying in a megalomaniacal, egocentric way, about forcing somebody to answer a question when you both know the answer already. Teachers do it. Policemen do it. Traffic policemen always bloody do it. 'Is there any particular reason that you were doing 123mph ... sir?'

And then they wait for an answer.

'Did you think that the speed limit didn't apply to you?'

And so on and so forth. The point of all this is not so that the copper in question can learn more about your motivations and beliefs. They lack such psychoanalytic curiosity. That's why they're traffic policemen. By making you answer a question to which they already know the answer, they are asserting their authority, and belittling yours. That's also why they're traffic policemen. That's also why such a series of questions is called subjectio.

It's a trick of which Mr Quentin Tarantino is inordinately fond and it makes myriad appearances in *Pulp Fiction*. There are subjectios about foot massages, Fonzies and driving. Subjectio is the centre of two of the most famous scenes. First, there is the great subjectio that begins, 'What does Marsellus Wallace look like?' To which, after a little shooting and stammering, we get the answer that he's black. Then that he's bald. And then comes the famous poser of: 'Does Marsellus Wallace look like a bitch?'

It is clear both from the baldness and the general context that Marsellus Wallace does not in the slightest bit resemble a bitch. And even someone who has never seen the film will already suspect that it's a mix-up rarely made. It's also clear that everybody in the room already knows exactly what Mr Wallace looks like. But the poor chap is made, with some more shooting, to answer in the negative. Which is how we come to the climactic question of the subjectio: 'Then why you trying to fuck him like a bitch?'

Is it possible to pigeonhole every type of rhetorical question? Not quite. Which is, perhaps, why the Ancients thought up so many terms to such little effect. Take this intricate enquiry from Inspector Harry Callahan (unwashed):

I know what you're thinking, punk. You're thinking 'Did he fire six shots or only five?' Now to tell you the truth I forgot myself in all this excitement. But being this is a .44 Magnum, the most powerful handgun in the world, and will blow your head clean

off, you've got to ask yourself a question: 'Do I feel lucky?' Well,
do you, punk?

Inspector Callahan was a master of the combined rhetorical
question. There seems to be an anthypophora, but it remains
unanswered so you could call it an erotesis. And then there's
the appeal to the interests of the audience (presuming that they
are interested in not getting their heads blown clean off), which
would be an odd sort of anacoenosis. And then we seem to end
with a subjectio where he requires an answer. But even then
there is ambiguity, because this line is used twice: at the beginning of the film and at the end of the film.

At the beginning there is a bank robbery and, after some
exciting shooting, all that's left is Harry Callahan with his maybe
loaded .44 Magnum in his hand and a bank robber with a definitely loaded shotgun just within reach. Mr Callahan weaves his
web of questions and the poor bank robber, of course, decides
that he is not feeling lucky. Thus it is subjectio.

At the end of the film Mr Callahan is faced with an almost
identical situation, except that the role of the bank robber is now
being filled by a giggling psychopath. Callahan repeats his lines
word for word; and the killer leaps for the gun.

So perhaps this is also a case of aporia.

Sometimes, people ask questions because they actually don't
know the answer. This works rhetorically. When Hamlet asks 'To
be or not to be' he doesn't just come down with a hypophoric
'To be!' Instead, he stops and thinks. He restates the question
as a choice between suffering slings and arrows or taking arms.
Then he lists the good points of death (ending heartaches and
natural shocks). Then he sees death's one bad point (the afterlife,

the fear of something after death). Then he comes to a sort of conclusion that as we don't know what happens when you die, it ain't worth the risk.[4]

Asking a question when you really don't know the answer is called aporia. It is the moment of doubt, when you're really not sure whether to top yourself.

The same sorts of doubt assailed poor Mr Presley when he sang 'Are You Lonesome Tonight?', a song whose melodic section consists only of rhetorical aporias.[5] Here, we must suppose that he really wants an answer. If she is lonesome tonight and her memory does stray to bright and osculatory summer days, then he's a happy man. If on the other hand she's got plenty of company tonight thank you very much, he's in trouble. Here, there is an answer, we just don't know what it is. *How do you do what you do to me? Will you still love me tomorrow? Who's that girl running around with you?*

And finally, there is the sort of rhetorical question that Bob Dylan used in 'Blowin' in the Wind'; the sort where there is no answer, the sort where the questioner does not know the answer, does not expect anyone else to know the answer, and does not expect to be informed. Bob Dylan knows that the answer, my friend, is blowing in the breeze; but he asks anyway. He does not expect to find how many roads a man must walk down. Anyway, it would probably depend on the length and location

---

[4] This is rather peculiar, as in Act I Hamlet's dad had appeared to him and explained exactly what happens after death, thus making Hamlet's great speech completely inconsistent with the plot of the play.

[5] The original recording of the song by Vaughan DeLeath in 1927 contains some explanatory verses. Elvis, though, cut these and sang entirely in questions. The original version does not contain the execrable spoken section.

of the roads, not to mention all the trouble of whether a street, alleyway or bridlepath can be taken into the count.

The same goes for William Blake's ponderings on the *Panthera tigris*, which go well beyond those of most naturalists. The poem does not have a full stop. It is all questions from beginning to end. But just as a prayer is a request to which you would be surprised to receive a yes or no, so Blake did not seriously expect a tiger to write him a letter answering the question:

Tiger, tiger, burning bright
In the forests of the night,
What immortal hand or eye
Dare frame thy fearful symmetry?

Though 'forests of the night' is a nice example of hendiadys. Probably.

Chapter 14

——⚬⚬⚬——

Hendiadys

Hendiadys (pronounced hen-DIE-a-dis) is the most elusive and tricky of all rhetorical tricks. Mostly because you can never be sure whether it's happened.

The principle of hendiadys is easy. You take an adjective and a noun, and then you change the adjective into another noun. So instead of saying 'I'm going to the noisy city' you say 'I'm going to the noise and the city'. Instead of saying 'I walked through the rainy morning' you say 'I walked through the rain and the morning'. Got it? The adjective-noun *noisy-city* becomes the noun-and-noun *noise and city*. Instead of saying 'I love your beautiful eyes' you say 'I love your beauty and eyes'.

But here's the problem. The writer knows that *beauty and eyes* meant *beautiful eyes*. But the reader doesn't know that. The poor reader might think that 'I love your beauty and eyes' means 'I love your beauty in general and your eyes in particular'.

So when Saint Paul told the Philippians to 'work out your salvation with fear and trembling', it's probably a hendiadys for *fearful trembling*, but it might be a hendiadys for *trembling fear*. And there's at least the possibility that he really did mean *both with fear and with trembling*, and wasn't using hendiadys at all.

Is *law and order* a hendiadys? It looks damned like it, but I would hate to say for certain. What about *rough and tumble*? *House and home*? To say for certain that something is hendiadys you have to be certain about what the writer thought in the first place. It may be that God has a glorious powerful kingdom, but Jesus actually said: 'For thine is the kingdom, and the power, and the glory'.[1]

Summertime living is easy. But *Summertime and the living is easy* doesn't necessarily have to be hendiadys. It just looks very, very like it.

There's also a variant form of hendiadys where adverb-adjective becomes adjective-adjective. If your tea is nice and hot and my champagne is nice and chilled, those would both appear to be hendiadyses for nicely hot and nicely chilled. But there is the possibility that my champagne is both nice – of good quality – and has been properly chilled.

There's also (some would say) the double verb form where you *try and do* something rather than *trying to do* something or *go and see* somebody rather than *going to see them*. And I would cheerily say that the forests of the night in which William Blake's tiger was burning bright are a hendiadys for forests at night.[2] But without summoning Mr Blake up from the dead, I'll never be able to prove it.

Another odd thing about hendiadys is that it's either common as muck or as rare as gold. Lots of everyday forgettable phrases use it (*be a good fellow and close the door* is not two commands). But almost no great writers do, except Shakespeare. Those lines listed above are almost the only examples in English

---

[1] Matthew's Gospel is in Greek and Jesus would have been speaking Aramaic. But hendiadys was a common form in Greek – in fact, it's a Greek word meaning 'two-for-one' – and the trick was also common in ancient Hebrew. So the possibility of hendiadys is definitely there.

[2] Some would object to this and call it antiptosis instead. I don't care. To English ears it sounds and feels just like a hendiadys, as, indeed, does 'She walks in beauty, like the night'.

literature, outside Shakespeare. And Shakespeare really only
used it for a few years. But those were the few years when he
wrote *Hamlet, Othello, Macbeth, Antony and Cleopatra* and *King
Lear*. That was the great period.

In Shakespeare's early works hendiadys barely appears.
Maybe popping up once or twice a play. Then, in about 1599,
Shakespeare appears to have had a moment and a revelation.
He suddenly decided that hendiadys was his favourite form. You
can draw a graph of the frequency[3] and watch it leap up, peak,
plateau, and drop away in what's usually called his late (and not
great) period. Now, I'm not arguing that hendiadys was the only
thing that made those five tragedies great, but it's worth noting that that's when he used the rhetorical form. *Hamlet* is the
top play, where he averages a hendiadys every 60 or so lines.
'Angels and ministers of grace defend us!' shouts Hamlet, when
he really means 'Angelic ministers of grace'. But obviously the
first thing you do when you see the ghost of your dead father
is employ a bit of hendiadys. Hamlet's father doesn't mind; he's
been too busy with the 'sulphurous and tormenting flames' of
purgatory (by which he means *tormentingly sulphurous*). Hamlet
notes all this down in the 'book and volume' of his brain. This
could mean *voluminous book* or *bookish volume* – that's one
of the wonderful things about hendiadys: it confuses things.
It takes something that might have been clear as an azure lake
in spring and muddies it. An English teacher will tell you that

---

[3] I have. I'm a lonely man. If you want to do your own you'll just need George T.
Wright's essay 'Hendiadys and Hamlet'. It's in PMLA, 1981, Vol. 96, Issue 2. Use
the table of figures for all Shakespeare's plays in Appendix II. You can use it to
impress your imaginary friends. You can also go for Schulze's list (1908) or Kerl's
(1922), but only if you speak German.

The Purpose Of The Adjective Is To Describe The Noun. One does a job for the other. Not in hendiadys and not in Shakespeare. Here you just get the nouns lined up, one beside the other, and though they're holding hands, you can't tell which is in charge. 'The morn and liquid dew of youth' is beautiful, but bewildering. So is 'the grace and blush of modesty', and 'the dead vast and middle of the night'.

And, of course, many times you can't quite work out if it's a hendiadys or not. Is it nobler in the mind to suffer the slings and arrows of outrageous fortune, or were they really the slung arrows, the arrows that fortune had hurled? Is flesh heir to 'the heartache and the thousand natural shocks' or to a thousand natural and heart-aching shocks? Do we bear 'the whips and scorns of time' or the scornful whips? Shakespeare was so frantic and keen on hendiadys when he was writing *Hamlet* that it could be lurking almost anywhere.

Hendiadys is hidden all over Shakespeare's great plays. It's in *King Lear* where Edmund says, 'I have told you what I have seen and heard; but faintly, nothing like the image and horror of it'; and, most famously, in *Macbeth*, where life is a tale 'Told by an idiot, full of sound and fury'. Whether Shakespeare was thinking of furious sound or sounding fury hardly signifies. The point and beauty of hendiadys is that it sets the words next to each other, that it removes the grammar and relation, that it doubles the words out to give breadth and beauty.

And then Shakespeare stopped using it. Nobody knows why, but hendiadys hardly appears in the late plays at all. Perhaps he thought better of it. Perhaps he got bored with it. Perhaps he regretted it. But for one little rhetorical trick to be the favourite of the greatest writer during his greatest period means that hendiadys has had its fifteen minutes and its fame.

Mind you, for my money, the greatest use of hendiadys isn't by Shakespeare, but by Leonard Cohen in his song 'Hallelujah':

You saw her bathing on the roof.
Her beauty and the moonlight overthrew you.

The 'and' where we might expect 'in' makes the hendiadys. And that whole song is, like so many songs, an extended example of epistrophe.

Chapter 15

Epistrophe

When you end each sentence with the same word, that's epistrophe. When each clause has the same words at the end, that's epistrophe. When you finish each paragraph with the same word, that's epistrophe. Even when it's a whole phrase or a whole sentence that you repeat, it's still, providing the repetition comes at the end, epistrophe.

This means that half the songs ever written are just extended examples of epistrophe. Whether it's Leonard Cohen ending every verse with *hallelujah*, Gershwin ending every clause with *the man I love* or Don McLean following each verse with a whole chorus of *Bye, bye, Miss American Pie* etc., that's epistrophe. When the moon hits your eye like a big pizza pie, that's also epistrophe because it always ends with amore.

In music epistrophe is so common that we barely notice it or think about it. We're all so familiar with the way songs work that we don't see that they work in a particular way. Because epistrophe brings with it some quite definite feelings. Wherever you start you always come back to the same thing. Wherever Bob Dylan starts off, he always ends up out there on Highway 61. Whatever is said in the verse, you can be sure that come the chorus everybody in the whole cell block will continue to dance to the jailhouse rock.

Epistrophe is the trope of obsession. It's the trope of emphasising one point again and again. And it's the trope of not being able to escape that one conclusion, which is one of the reasons that songs are so suited to the idea of obsessive love, political certainty and other such unhealthy ideas. You can't reason in an epistrophic pop song. You can't seriously consider the alternatives, because the structure dictates that you'll always end up at the same point, thinking about the same girl and giving peace a chance. Wherever you are in the world and whatever question Bob asks, you already know that you'll be dancing in the street while the answer blows in the wind. It's built into the structure. It's epistrophe.

When the music stops, epistrophe can get a little more subtle. It can be merely emphatic, a kind of banging on the table, jabbing at the air for emphasis. That's the sort that Abraham Lincoln used when he said 'government of the people, by the people, for the people, shall not perish from the earth'. I'm pretty sure that there would have been a hand gesture repeated for each *people*. The same goes for Othello as he says, 'A fine woman! a fair woman! a sweet woman!', or Shylock with, 'I'll have my bond! Speak not against my bond! / I have sworn an oath that I will have my bond.' It's also the sort of useful reminder when a witness promises to tell the truth, the whole truth and nothing but the truth. And it's the sort of threatening bluster when, in *The Treasure of the Sierra Madre*, a bandit leader refuses to prove that he's a policeman: 'Badges? We ain't got no badges. We don't need no badges! I don't have to show you any stinkin' badges!'

But those are the quick epistrophes, the single-clause epistrophes, the emphasis epistrophes. Epistrophe gets bigger and stronger the longer you delay it. Probably the most famous example of this in modern rhetoric is Barack Obama's various epistrophic speeches, in which he always ended up with *Yes we can*. He leaves whole paragraphs of American history between them, but he always ends up with the same answer. Whatever the obstacle, whatever the objection, the answer is always the same. Yes we can.[1]

It's the same hopeful, cheer-every-repetition formula that made the greatest speech in the 1939 novel *The Grapes of Wrath* by John Steinbeck:

> Wherever there's a fight so hungry people can eat, I'll be there. Wherever there's a cop beating up a guy, I'll be there. I'll be in the way guys yell when they're mad and – I'll be in the way kids laugh when they're hungry and they know supper's ready. And when our folk eat the stuff they raise and live in the houses they build – why, I'll be there.

But these ideas don't really get to the heart of epistrophe. They use it, but they don't inhabit it. Because epistrophe, usually, by its very form, has an underlying sense of *No you can't*. Whatever you try to do, however you start out, you'll always end up at the same place, back where you started, as with the songs above. It just so happens that Mr Obama's starting point was *Yes we can*. But epistrophe is much more natural when you're in trouble. When Henry V has traitors brought before him, he says:

> Show men dutiful?
> Why, so didst thou: seem they grave and learned?
> Why, so didst thou: come they of noble family?
> Why, so didst thou: seem they religious?
> Why, so didst thou.

---

[1] It is a principle and rhetorical trick you should never teach to small children.

And you know he's angry. You know that they aren't getting out of this one. And indeed they don't get out of this one. Henry executes the lot of them. Wherever you start out, you're going to finish up with *so didst thou*. And whatever they say, their necks are marked for the chopping block.

In fact, epistrophe is particularly suited for death; I suppose because death is the huge human epistrophe, and all biographies end the same way. Thus the technique seems so suitable in Psalm 118 where we run through a list of nations and people and find, in each case, that 'in the name of the Lord, I will destroy them'. Epistrophe is probably at its most natural in the film *Lock, Stock and Two Smoking Barrels*,[2] where an angry gang boss explains his terms to a rather unfortunate fellow who's accidentally crossed him.

> If you hold back anything, I'll kill you. If you bend the truth, or I think you're bending the truth, I'll kill you. If you forget anything, I'll kill you. In fact, you're going to have to work very hard to stay alive, Nick. Now, do you understand everything I've said? Because if you don't, I'll kill you.

Death is an epistrophe and epistrophe is death. But …

Epistrophe works wonderfully with a good *but*. You demonstrate that all the doors are closed. This door is closed. That door is closed. The other door is closed. And then you point out the fire exit.

It's used a little clumsily by Aragorn in the film of *The Lord of the Rings: The Return of the King* when he tells everyone that:

---

[2] By Mr Guy Ritchie, released in 1998.

A day may come when the courage of men fails, when we forsake our friends and break all bonds of fellowship, but it is not this day. An hour of woes and shattered shields, when the age of men comes crashing down! But it is not this day! This day we fight!

Slightly better is Saint Paul who finds himself in an epistrophe and then, inevitably, finds his way out:

When I was a child, I spake as a child, I understood as a child, I thought as a child: but when I became a man, I put away childish things. For now we see through a glass, darkly; but then face to face: now I know in part; but then shall I know even as also I am known. And now abideth faith, hope, love, these three; but the greatest of these is love.

Faith, hope and love is a good example of a tricolon.

Chapter 16

Tricolon

I came; I saw; I conquered.
Sun, sea and sex.

Three is the magic number of literary composition, but to explain why that is you have to look at the much more boring number two.

Whenever the average human sees two things together, they connect them. So if I say the words *eat and drink*, you will, unless you're a bit weird, notice that those are the two major forms of ingestion.[1] You might also see eat and drink as opposites: solid vs. liquid. The same thought will occur to you if I mention the father and the son or the good and the bad or truth and justice.

Even if we take two things that don't fit together we'll find something. Mice and men? Well, they're … they're small and big? Cabbages and kings? One is familiar and domestic and the other grand and distant? That's just how the human brain is built, and it's all the fault of God and Darwin. We see a pair and we see a pattern.

You can always, always connect two dots with a straight line.

---

[1] There was a brief nineteenth-century fad for putting food up your bottom. President James Garfield was fed this way for a month. Then he died. For information you may consult *Feeding Per Rectum* by Doctor William Bliss (1882). The colon and the tricolon do not, unfortunately, have even an etymological connection.

But add another word and they're tricolons. Eat, drink and be merry. Father, Son and Holy Spirit. The Good, the Bad and the Ugly. Truth, justice and the American way.

With a tricolon you can set up a pattern and then break it. 'Lies, damned lies, and statistics' is a simple example. The first two words establish the direction we're going. The third twists things for humorous purposes. This is, incidentally, the structure of a particular kind of joke. Did you hear the one about three people in a peculiar situation? The first two do something sensible, but the third does something really odd! It doesn't matter whether you populate it with priests and rabbis, or with Englishmen, Irishmen and Scotsmen; it's always the same basic joke.

The surprise can be based purely on sound. Alliteration provides the twist of 'Wine, women and song' and rhyme gives it to 'Ready, steady, go'.

Or the surprise can simply be for the sake of surprise. 'It's a bird! It's a plane! It's Superman!' The famous *Superman* opening is a whirl of tricolons, and tricolons planted within tricolons. It begins with a surprise one, and it ends with an extender: truth, justice and the American way.[2]

Tricolons sound great if the third thing is longer. The American way is (as outlined in their mutinous Declaration of Independence) made up of life, liberty and the pursuit of happiness. The pursuit of happiness is, if you think about it, the least of the promises here. You can pursue happiness as much as you like, and most of us do anyway. It rarely ends in capture. Life and liberty were the more important guarantees. But it sounds

---

[2] I suppose this might be classed as a surprise tricolon by politically active, sincere, tedious people.

so good when you go on a bit at the end. 'Friends, Romans, countrymen' works the same way. In terms of content Antony would have been much better off starting with the fact that they're all of the same nationality, then pointing out that they are Romans, and finally, in a gushy sort of way, pointing out that they are really friends too. But the longest bit of the tricolon must be saved for last, even if it's the least important. Lady Caroline Lamb knew this when she called Byron 'Mad, bad and dangerous to know'. And Shakespeare knew it when he wrote: 'We few, we happy few, we band of brothers', or 'of graves, of worms and epitaphs', or ... when it comes to tricolons, Shakespeare had been there, done that, and bought the T-shirt.

In fact, there's something nasty, brutish and short[3] about some tricolons, which just punch you with three words. The French should have seen where the revolution would end up when it got the motto *Liberté, Egalité, Fraternité*. That's dictatorship right there. The Germans got shorter still with *Ein Reich! Ein Volk! Ein Führer!* and sent all their *Fräuleins* off to look after the *Kinder, Küche, Kirche*.

Sometimes the tricolon goes in exactly the direction you expected, but this is actually rather rare. There's Rick in *Casablanca* complaining about 'all the gin-joints, in all the towns, in all the world', and there's Douglas Adams' great question of 'life, the universe, and everything'. But lengthening and surprise are much more important and much more powerful.

Another problem with the rising tricolon is that it has to get to the end. When you go up, you can't stop halfway. That's why

---

[3] Hobbes' original line was 'the life of man, solitary, poor, nasty, brutish and short' but memory has corrected the number.

Rick has to get to the realistic upper limit of the world, and the galactic hitchhiker to the preposterous upper limit of everything. Two's company, three's a list, and a list has to be complete.

That's the final and most important aspect of the tricolon. The good and the bad together make up two sides of the moral coin. The Good, the Bad and the Ugly is a list of the major characters in a film. Eat and drink are two methods of ingestion. Eat, drink and be merry is a list of all the things you need to do this evening. Father and son is a generational pair: Father, Son and Holy Ghost is a list of all the aspects of God. When you finish a tricolon, you finish because there is nothing more to say. You've said it all. The list is complete. These are the final words.

This sense of completeness makes the tricolon perfectly suited to grand rhetoric. That's why Barack Obama packed 21 tricolons into his short victory speech. Tricolons sound statesmanlike. It's government of the people, by the people, for the people. Even though only a whip-smart listener would see the difference between 'of the people' and 'by the people', it doesn't matter. It's three and three sounds good.

Two is only a pair, and four is all wrong. Churchill tried a four (it's called a tetracolon). In his first speech to Parliament as Prime Minister he told them that he had 'nothing to offer but blood, toil, tears and sweat'. But four doesn't work and everybody remembers the line as 'blood, sweat and tears'.[4]

---

[4] The origins of this phrase are rather complicated. Churchill never said 'blood, sweat and tears' but Theodore Roosevelt did in 1897, and Lord Alfred Douglas said 'Blood and sweat and tears' in 1919. However, my point here is that everybody remembers it as a Churchill line, or, more precisely, misremembers that Churchill line by making it a tricolon. Also, Churchill never said 'Rum, sodomy and the lash'.

It is always three and never four. Estate agents do not rely on the rule location, location, location, location, although that would still be an example of epizeuxis.

Chapter 17

—∞∞∞—

Epizeuxis

This book is about one tiny, tiny aspect of rhetoric: the figures of speech. There are all sorts of other bits to the subject: arguing, proving, inventing, memorising, and delivery. When an Ancient Greek chap was learning rhetoric he even had to learn the correct hand gestures, or *actions*, to be used at different points in the speech. The great orator Demosthenes was once asked what the three most important things in rhetoric were, and he replied: 'Action. Action. Action.'

History does not record how he gestured as he said this. He may have punched the air or twiddled his thumbs. All we know is what he said, and how he said it: with epizeuxis.

Epizeuxis (pronounced ep-ee-ZOOX-is) is repeating a word immediately in exactly the same sense. Simple. Simple. Simple. However, epizeuxis is not the easiest way to get into the dictionary of quotations. It's like a nuclear bomb: immensely effective, but a bit weird if you use it every five minutes.

Demosthenes was using epizeuxis for the very old joke of enumerating the same thing. Twenty-three centuries later it was still being used in lines like: 'The first rule of Fight Club is: you do not talk about Fight Club. The second rule of Fight Club is: you do not talk about Fight Club.'[1] But the pure epizeuxis form

---

[1] From the film *Fight Club* (1999), surprisingly, by Chuck Palahniuk (novel) and Jim Uhls (screenplay).

is still around as well. Since the 1920s it has been a maxim of American real estate agents that the three most important things about a property are 'location, location, location'. In 1996 Tony Blair told the Labour Party conference: 'Ask me my three main priorities for government and I tell you: education, education and education.' Mr Blair had, almost certainly, stolen the joke from real estate agents, but it goes back to Demosthenes.

'Education, education, education' got the biggest round of applause and the best headlines of the party conference, which is probably why Blair decided to try epizeuxis again three months later during Prime Minister's questions. He wasn't Prime Minister at the time, instead poor John Major was in charge and trying to control the wild and bloodthirsty menagerie commonly known as the Conservative Party. Tony Blair said: 'Isn't it extraordinary that the Prime Minister of our country can't even urge his Party to back his own position? Weak! Weak! Weak!' And again he hit the headlines, but this time the three words were being used not as the Demosthenian joke: this was epizeuxis for intensification.

Back in 1994 Tony Blair told an interviewer that 'The art of leadership is saying no', a point that he had probably learnt from Margaret Thatcher. She outlined her position on Europe to the House of Commons with three words: 'No. No. No.' It so happens that in the context of the debate she was answering three rather precise points made by Jacques Delors, the President of the European Commission. The full line reads like this:

'The President of the Commission, M. Delors, said at a press conference the other day that he wanted the European Parliament to be the democratic body of the Community, he wanted the Commission to be the Executive and he wanted the Council of Ministers to be the Senate. No. No. No.'

But all that's remembered is the emphatic epizeuxis of 'No. No. No.', where the repetition is no numerical joke, but a sign of emotion, conviction and emphasis, just as in *Macbeth* you have, 'O horror, horror, horror', and in *King Lear*, 'Howl! Howl! Howl! Howl!' King Lear is here breaking the golden rule of three, which is a sign, I suppose, of his madness. His last speech is an exercise in epizeuxis:

> And my poor fool is hang'd! No, no, no life!
> Why should a dog, a horse, a rat, have life,
> And thou no breath at all? Thou'lt come no more,
> Never, never, never, never, never!
> Pray you, undo this button: thank you, sir.
> Do you see this? Look on her, look, her lips,
> Look there, look there!
> [*Dies*]

There is a popular story that Henry VIII died on an epizeuxis. He is meant to have gazed into the dark corners of the room and shrieked 'Monks! Monks! Monks!' It's complete nonsense and seems to have been dreamt up in the mid-nineteenth century, but the story has survived because it sounds right. In fact, Henry VIII was speechless on his deathbed and only managed, apparently, to squeeze the Archbishop of Canterbury's hand when asked if he trusted in God. Perhaps, though, the monks would have been even more dramatic had they been mumbled.

Epizeuxis is ambiguous. Sometimes it means a moment of intense emotion, and sometimes an inescapable drone. The actor playing King Lear can either scream the words 'Never, never, never, never, never!' or mumble them. He can't do much in between. Repetition can mean … repetition, repetition, repetition on and on and on and on for ever and ever. 'Tomorrow and tomorrow and tomorrow / Creeps in this petty pace from day to day' is clearly a case of a man resigning himself to the dull, inevitable future. The same resignation of Alfred Lord Tennyson watching the waves and saying: 'Break, break, break, / On thy cold grey stones, O Sea!'

This quieter form of epizeuxis can even be dismissive. When Polonius asks Hamlet what he's reading, Hamlet replies, 'Words, words, words' in a way that implies perhaps only a shrug. And maybe that the book is too long. It's the same bored condescension that was implied by Prince William, Duke of Gloucester when he was presented with the second volume of Gibbon's *Decline and Fall of the Roman Empire*: 'Another damned thick book! Always scribble, scribble, scribble! Eh, Mr Gibbon?'

Other forms of epizeuxis are less powerful. Without the rule of three, epizeuxis loses its punch. The only really great double is 'The horror! The horror!' in Conrad's *Heart of Darkness*. Mid-sentence, the double does not do much more than add a bit of emphasis – 'I'm shocked, *shocked* to find that gambling is going on in here' – but it's very, very rare.

At the beginning of a sentence epizeuxis has rather more power. 'Tiger, tiger, burning bright', 'Rage, rage against the dying of the light', 'Gone, gone again'.

'My God, my God, why hast thou forsaken me?' asked Jesus on the cross. And a few years later, clearly pleased with the effect, he struck down Saul on the road to Damascus and asked, 'Saul, Saul, why persecutest thou me?', which seems an odd thing to ask of somebody that you've just struck down and blind, but there we are.

'Striking down and blind' is, by the way, an example of syllepsis.

Chapter 18

---⊗⊗⊗---

Syllepsis

Syllepsis is when one word is used in two incongruous ways. In fact, it can be more than two. Let's start with nine, which is the longest example I've ever found. There is an old (and doubtless untrue) story of a young journalist who was criticised by his editor for not being brief enough. His articles, he was told, had Too Many Words. The next day, he filed this report:

> A shocking affair occurred last night. Sir Edward Hopeless, as guest at Lady Panmore's ball, complained of feeling ill, took a highball, his hat, his coat, his departure, no notice of his friends, a taxi, a pistol from his pocket, and finally his life. Nice chap. Regrets and all that.

The verb *took* is applied to nine different nouns in a way that seems rather absurd. We all take no notice of things, and sometimes we take taxis, and occasionally we take our own lives, but generally in English we don't do them in one sentence. It makes the word *took* look rather silly. Or rather it makes us think about the many ways that we can use the verb. It also sounds rather funny when a noun as commonplace as *hat* is, by grammar, made equal with a noun like *life*.

In its simplest form syllepsis is just a pun. There's a story that Dorothy Parker once commented on her small apartment, saying: 'I've barely room enough to lay my hat and a few friends.'

There are all sorts of slightly different ways that syllepsis can work. There's a wonderful thing called a phrasal verb. Essentially it's a verb plus a preposition, which together give you a whole new meaning: for example, *doing up a house*. A foreigner learning English might know the word *do* and the word *up*, but would still be unable to work out why you were *performing a building skywards*. And when he discovered that you could also *do in* your enemies, he would be *done for*.

'Muck out' means to clean a stable, 'muck in' to help, to 'muck about' is to play uselessly and to 'muck up' is to ruin. So a lazy and incompetent stable hand could be said to muck about constantly, out and in rarely, and up everything. It's on this principle that Rosamond Lehmann complained of her fellow novelist Ian Fleming: 'The trouble with Ian is that he gets off with women because he can't get on with them.'

Or you can use the verb plain and the verb phrasal in one sentence. There's a song called 'Have Some Madeira M'Dear', which contains long lines of syllepsis like 'she made no reply, up her mind, and a dash for the door'.

But the commonest form is the simple contrast of the concrete and the abstract. When the prophet Joel told the people of Israel to 'Rend your heart, and not your garments' he was using the same trick that the prophet Mick Jagger[1] employed when he talked in one song about a lady who was able to blow not only his nose, but his mind, although for rather different purposes. Indeed, one suspects that Mr Jagger was planning another syllepsis based on *blow* that would have got the song banned on radio.

---

[1] The song – 'Honky Tonk Women' – is credited to Jagger/Richards.

There's something ridiculous about syllepsis, which is probably what attracted Lewis Carroll to it. Lines like:

> You may seek it with thimbles – and seek it with care;
>   You may hunt it with forks and hope;
> You may threaten its life with a railway-share;
>   You may charm it with smiles and soap.

It can also make you look very clever (usually while it makes others look ridiculous). Syllepsis was a favourite of the poet Alexander Pope. He loved combining the abstract with the concrete to make others look silly. A girl might 'Lose her heart or honour at a ball' or 'Stain her honour or her new brocade'. He even used it to make fun of Queen Anne:

> Here Thou, great Anna! whom three Realms obey,
> Dost sometimes Counsel take – and sometimes Tea.

(It should be noted that, when Pope wrote that, *tea* was pronounced *tay* and rhymed with *obey*.) Syllepsis was also a favourite of Charles Dickens, who wrote lines like: 'Mr Pickwick took his hat and his leave', or 'He fell into a barrow, and fast asleep'. Indeed, for my money, Dickens wrote the most splendid syllepsis in England with: 'Miss Bolo rose from the table considerably agitated, and went straight home, in a flood of tears, and a sedan chair.'

But the advantages of syllepsis are also its failings. Syllepsis makes the reader astonished and go back to check what the word was and how it's working now. It's terribly witty, but it's terribly witty in a look-at-me-aren't-I-witty sort of way. There's a sense in which it's a cheap thrill. When Alanis Morissette sings 'You held your breath and the door for me'[2] you can either marvel at her rhetorical deftness or turn up your nose and off the radio. Syllepsis can get out of hand, up your nose, on your nerves and used too much.

There are, though, subtle syllepses. 'Make love not war' is a syllepsis, just one that's barely noticeable. It gives the phrase its spice, but you wouldn't be able to pick out the flavour without a good long chew. The same goes in a sense for 'Tea and Sympathy' or the two boys in *Tom Sawyer* who 'covered themselves in dust and glory'. These tiny syllepses hide all over the place. The reader likes the line, remembers the line, but doesn't know why.

Nobody seriously believes that aviaries anger an omnipotent and ferocious being. If we did believe that, we wouldn't have aviaries. It's an insane thought. Nonetheless, William Blake is still in print saying:

> A robin redbreast in a cage
> Puts all Heaven in a rage.

Why? Because the third stressed syllable of each line is 'in'. The first time, the *in* is physical, the second time it is abstract. And the result is a couplet with no theological or logical backing, which has nonetheless survived for hundreds of years. The subtle disorientation of the syllepsis, and the neatness of the rhyme, makes us believe in something that we would scoff at were it phrased in any other way by any other animal rights activist.

---

[2] 'Head Over Feet' (1996) by Alanis Morissette and Glen Ballard.

Somewhere in a Californian hotel there are, according to the Eagles, mirrors *on the ceiling*. There is also pink champagne *on ice*. The first *on* is the normal *attached to*, the second is a special colloquial usage. It's like being 'out of your mind and out of a job', but so much softer. There's just enough of a shift to prick the listener's ears up. If the line had been 'Mirrors on the ceiling and champagne on the bar' it wouldn't be half as memorable. But it would still be a good example of isocolon.

Chapter 19

Isocolon

Roses are red.
Violets are blue.

That, at its simplest, is isocolon. Two clauses that are grammatically parallel, two sentences that are structurally the same. The Ancient Greeks were rather obsessed with isocolon, the modern world has rather forgotten it. The Greeks loved the sense of balance that it gave to writing, which reflected the sense of balance that they admired in thought. With isocolon one seems reasonable; without isocolon one seems hasty. With isocolon language acquired a calm rhythm, without isocolon prose became a formless heap. On the one hand the figure could describe antithesis with its graceful contrasts, on the other hand the trick could show emphasis through its gentle repetitions. O for the classical balance! Woe to the modern mess!

Because though isocolon can still be used in the calm Greek manner, it usually isn't. When Cassius Clay said 'Float like a butterfly, sting like a bee', he had no calm and peaceful thoughts in his mind. And when Rick tells Ilsa, 'Where I'm going, you can't follow. What I've got to do, you can't be any part of', he doesn't sound like Socrates contemplating virtue, he sounds like a man in a crisis with a gun and a girl at an airport.

Modern isocolons tend to work as a kind of spot-the-difference game. We use the similarities to point up the differences, and use the differences to point up the similarities. Rick's lines contrast *where* with *what*, *going* with *doing*, *following* with *taking part*. So the sentences are differentiated: the first is about geographical movement, the second is about physical action. But at the same time the sentences simply restate each other. The 'I' and the 'you can't' remain in their places, and Rick and Ilsa part at the airport.

Similarity and difference, comparison and contrast, are the stock in trade of isocolon, and that's how Shakespeare liked to use it. When Brutus is explaining why he killed Julius Caesar, he gives this reply:

As Caesar loved me, I weep for him; as he was fortunate, I rejoice at it; as he was valiant, I honour him: but, as he was ambitious, I slew him. There is tears for his love; joy for his fortune; honour for his valour; and death for his ambition.

This is obviously a much more extended case of isocolon. You don't have to stop at two parallels, you can go on for a very long time, so long as your lungs are big enough. John F. Kennedy in his inauguration address announced:

Let every nation know, whether it wishes us well or ill, that we shall pay any price, bear any burden, meet any hardship, support any friend, oppose any foe, to assure the survival and the success of liberty.

And Winston Churchill beat that with the slightly ridiculous:

> Fill the armies, rule the air, pour out the munitions, strangle the U-boats, sweep the mines, plough the land, build the ships, guard the streets, succour the wounded, uplift the downcast, and honour the brave.

This also shows up isocolon's weakness: people can hear it happening and it can all start to sound rather forced and artificial. Silly even. It's very hard to work an extended isocolon in subtly. It's strictly for the moment when you're addressing the crowds in Rome or Washington, or trying to win the Second World War over the radio. It's not the sort of trick you can use down the pub or try over dinner. If you do, Shakespeare makes fun of you thus:

> I praise God for you, sir: your reasons at dinner have been sharp and sententious; pleasant without scurrility, witty without affection, audacious without impudency, learned without opinion, and strange without heresy.

Much better to keep isocolons short and snappy. Float like a butterfly, sting like a bee, chat like a human being. Thus you can keep to the twin powers of isocolon: antitheses like 'Marry in haste, repent at leisure'; and restatements like 'Thy kingdom come, thy will be done'.

The isocolon is particularly useful to advertisers. The parallelism can imply that two statements are the same thing even if they aren't. 'Have a break. Have a Kit-Kat' is a clever little line because it uses isocolon to try to make two rather different things synonymous. The same goes for 'The future's bright. The future's Orange'.

Isocolon is also littered throughout the lyrics of pop music and the words of hymns.

> Morning has broken, like the first morning.
> Blackbird has spoken, like the first bird.

Melodies tend to repeat themselves, and so the words that are sung over them repeat themselves too. Sometimes these lines even conform to the ultra-strict definition of isocolon in the *Rhetorica ad Herennium*:[1] that the two clauses have exactly the same number of syllables.

But mostly our isocolons are heard, not counted; sensed, not defined. It is the wit of Churchill describing Field Marshal Montgomery as 'In defeat, unbeatable; in victory, unbearable'. Or it's the finality of 'Ashes to ashes, dust to dust'. Or it's the simplicity of 'You pays your money and you takes your choice'.

Which is also an example of enallage.

---

[1] The *Rhetorica ad Herennium* is the standard classical work on rhetoric, and contains all the strictest definitions. But see Epilogue, p. 203.

Chapter 20

Enallage

Enallage (e-NALL-aj-ee) is a deliberate grammatical mistake. That definition raises all sorts of philosophical questions about whether a mistake can be deliberate, and all sorts of linguistic questions about what correct English grammar is and whether one chap ever really has the right to tell another chap he's wrong. So perhaps it would be better to say that enallage is when a phrase stands out because of its unusual grammar. Simples.

At the end of *Heart of Darkness*, as they sail slowly back down the mysterious river ...

> ... the manager's boy put his insolent black head in the doorway, and said in a tone of scathing contempt—
> 'Mistah Kurtz – he dead.'

Joseph Conrad knew that grammatically a verb was required to make a complete sentence, but the line 'Mr Kurtz is dead' would have been neither striking nor memorable. It wouldn't have made the dictionary of quotations and T.S. Eliot wouldn't have used it as the epigraph for 'The Hollow Men'. *Heart of Darkness* is 39,000 words long, but everybody remembers those four. It's the bad grammar what makes the phrase. That enallage.

But though Conrad, the novelist, may make his mistakes intentionally, Joe Jacobs, the boxing manager, probably did not.

He made the dictionary of quotations[1] with an angry enallage. After his boxer Max Schmeling lost on points, Jacobs shouted to anybody who would listen that 'We was robbed'. Had his grammar been any better, Mr Jacobs would be forgotten.

And sometimes it is a little hard to say whether the enallage was deliberate or not. T.S. Eliot certainly knew the English language. He knew that *we* means *you and I* and that *us* means *you and me*. But he still started 'The Love Song of J. Alfred Prufrock'[2] with the words:

Let us go then, you and I,

Let I go?

Of course, it may just have been there to rhyme with *sky* in the next line. I'll never be sure and I can't ask him now. Most people don't notice the problem. But I have a theory that it's that little enallage, pricking away at the unconscious, that has made the line so famous.

Or maybe it was just the rhyme. After all, Shakespeare did it, using the same substitution.

Unless you would devise some virtuous lie,
To do more for me than mine own desert,
And hang more praise upon deceased I
Than niggard truth would willingly impart:

And nobody says Shakespeare couldn't write.

---

[1] *Bartlett's Familiar Quotations.*
[2] From *Collected Poems 1909–1962* by T.S. Eliot, published by Faber and Faber Ltd.

Strict grammarians don't seem to mind about the line 'Love me tender' either. Any child could tell you that the words should be 'love me tenderly, love me truly', but they aren't and it's much better that way. The chap who wrote those lyrics, Ken Darby, had the tune to contend with. It's an old Civil War melody that was originally about a girl called Aura Lea, and Darby had to make his lines fit. *Tenderly* and *truly* would have added another note to the end of the tune. If this was what happened, then, just as Eliot could point at Shakespeare, Darby could finger Dylan Thomas' 'Do not go gentle into that good night' or Alexander Pope's 'Hope springs eternal in the human breast'. In both cases the poor poets were just trying to fit their thoughts into verse, and if that meant they had to drop a 'ly', then so be it.

Chapter 21

A Divagation Concerning Versification

English verse is a reasonably simple business. Each English word has a stress on it. When a beggar starts work, he needs to begin beggin'. *Begin* has the stress on the second syllable – beGIN – and *beggin'* has the stress on the first – BEGgin'. The same thing goes with the verb *to rebel* and the noun *a rebel*. A REBel ReBELS. When you give a gift, you preSENT a PREsent. The only difference between the words is the stress.

Every word in English has a particular stress, and when a foreigner gets it wrong we notice, and we snigger. There's an old joke with many variations all of which involve a Frenchman in pursuit of a penis, rather than happiness. That's partially because the French don't pronounce their Hs, but mainly because HAPPiness and a PENis are stressed differently.

Some words even get two stresses. Antidote goes TUM-te-TUM. UNDerSTANDing goes TUM-te-TUM-te. And sometimes the stress is optional. You usually say HAPPiness, but you can, if you like, say HAPPinESS.

Also, even when a sentence is made out of words of one syllable, some will be stressed and some won't. 'A cup of tea' will always be stressed 'a CUP of TEA'. (Unless, I suppose, you're asked whether you wanted two cups next to tea, in which case you might reply, 'No, I want A cup OF tea'.)

So 'a lovely cup of tea' goes te-TUM-te-TUM-te-TUM. 'I want a lovely cup of tea' goes te-TUM-te-TUM-te-TUM-te-TUM.

'I really want a lovely cup of tea' goes te-TUM-te-TUM-te-TUM-te-TUM-te-TUM. And now you've got a rhythm going.

'Compare' is a te-TUM. 'Summer' is a TUM-te. So 'Shall I compare thee to a summer's day' goes te-TUM-te-TUM-te-TUM-te-TUM-te-TUM. And the next line, 'Thou art more lovely and more temperate', goes exactly the same way. 'Rough winds do shake the darling buds of May' is the same. 'And summer's lease hath all too short a date' is the same. Five te-TUMS in a row. Try reading those lines out while tapping your finger on something to keep time.

In verse a te-TUM is called an iamb, and five in a row is called a pentameter (that's the same *pent* as pentagon). So five te-TUMs are called an iambic pentameter.

Of course, there are lots of other ways that you can write. The iamb is just one of the four basic feet:

Iamb – te-TUM
Trochee – TUMty
Anapaest – te-te-TUM
Dactyl – TUM-te-ty

And the pentameter is one of the three basic meters:

Pentameter – five in a row
Tetrameter – four in a row
Trimeter – three in a row

So you can pick one from each list, and you've got yourself a verse form. Choose anapaest and tetrameter and you've got:

te-te-TUM te-te-TUM te-te-TUM te-te-TUM

Which Byron used for:

> The As<u>sy</u>rian came <u>down</u> like a <u>wolf</u> on the <u>fold</u>
> And his <u>co</u>horts were <u>glea</u>ming in <u>purp</u>le and <u>gold</u>

There are only twelve combinations, and they've all been tried a few times. And people have even gone off into the more obscure feet and lengths. Obviously the meters don't have to be just three, four and five. You can do anything from one up to infinity, if you feel like it. And there are all sorts of other strange feet like the choriamb (TUM-te-te-TUM) and the molossus (TUM! TUM! TUM!). But these strange ones have never really worked well in English apart from the amphibrach (te-TUM-te), which is the basis of the limerick:

> There <u>was</u> a young <u>man</u> from Cal<u>cut</u>ta

But I digress. The point is that even with the basic feet and the basic meters there are still only two or three combinations that actually get a lot of use. Anapaests and dactyls tend to sound a bit silly. Byron made the anapaest serious, but that's because he was an absolutely bloody amazing poet. If you try it yourself you'll probably end up with something that sounds like a nursery rhyme, because anapaests and dactyls are the nursery rhyme feet and they tend to sound rather higgledy piggledy wiggledy woo. 'Little Miss Muffet, she sat on a tuffet …'

The trochee doesn't sound silly, but it does sound a bit like a hammer, banging away. So Henry Wadsworth Longfellow's 1855 poem, *The Song of Hiawatha*, which is all in trochees, goes like this:

> By the shores of Gitche Gumee,
> By the shining Big-Sea-Water,

Stood the wigwam of Nokomis,
Daughter of the Moon, Nokomis.
Dark behind it rose the forest,
Rose the black and gloomy pine-trees,
Rose the firs with cones upon them;
Bright before it beat the water,
Beat the clear and sunny water,
Beat the shining Big-Sea-Water.

I mean it's effective. But it's a bit obvious. And remember that Hiawatha is an *epic* poem. After a while it feels as though there are builders working in your head.

Hiawatha actually made the trochee fashionable, something that doesn't ordinarily happen to metrical units. In November 1855 the gossip column of the *New York Times* claimed: 'The madness of the hour takes the metrical shape of trochees, everybody writes trochaics, talks trochaics, and thinks in trochees', which would drive me mad. Mind you, it's possible that everybody *was* talking in trochees. It's insanely simple once you get the rhythm in your head. Most people can improvise in unrhymed dactyls for hours. It's just that you lose all your friends if you do.

And that, as the bishop remarked to the crocodile, leaves us with only one foot: the iamb. The soft and lovely iamb. The humble te-TUM. Because the TUM falls on the offbeat, as it were, the rhythm is gentler. It never has the primeval power of the trochee, but nor does it have any of its primeval coarseness. The iamb is just the gentle rhythm, the waves lapping in the background.

The only question that remains is how many? The simplest answer is the greedy one. Four *and* three alternating: the tetrameter and the trimeter. This is called the ballad meter and it sounds wonderfully traditional.

> There is a house in New Orleans
> They call The Rising Sun
> It's been the ruin of many a poor boy
> In God, I know I'm one.

You probably noticed that the third line there isn't quite right. There are three soft syllables between *man-* and *boy*. That's all right for two reasons. First, there's slurring. *Many a* can be pronounced as *men-yer*. Give it a go. *Men-yer poor boy*. So that brings it down to only two soft syllables. What's *poor* doing there? Well, the truth is that once you've established a rhythm you can vary it a bit. It even makes the ballad meter sound more traditional. Rather like wonky timbers on an old building. They look good, and as long as it's all structurally sound, the more wonk the better. Here's the opening of *The Rime of the Ancient Mariner*:

> It is an ancient Mariner,
> And he stoppeth one of three.
> 'By thy long grey beard and glittering eye,
> Now wherefore stopp'st thou me?'

It's so damned folksy, and it's those extra syllables here and there that make it seem so rough and ready. You can, of course, write in pure ballad meter, and it sounds a lot more respectable.

> Because I could not stop for Death—
> He kindly stopped for me—
> The Carriage held but just Ourselves—
> And Immortality.

But it still has something of the nursery rhyme:

> 'The <u>time</u> has <u>come</u>,' the <u>Wal</u>rus <u>said</u>,
> 'To <u>talk</u> of <u>many</u> <u>things</u>:
> Of <u>shoes</u>—and <u>ships</u>—and <u>sealing-wax</u>—
> Of <u>cabbages</u>—and <u>kings</u>—
> And <u>why</u> the <u>sea</u> is <u>boiling</u> <u>hot</u>—
> And <u>whether</u> <u>pigs</u> have <u>wings</u>.'

It can always be sung to the tune of 'The House of the Rising Sun' or 'O Little Town of Bethlehem'. Nonetheless, you'll be even more dignified if you move up to the straight iambic tetrameter: te-TUM te-TUM te-TUM te-TUM.

The iambic tetrameter can do all sorts of things, but it's best at being sad and lyrical.

> I <u>wandered</u> <u>lonely</u> <u>as</u> a <u>Cloud</u>
> That <u>floats</u> on <u>high</u> o'er <u>Vales</u> and <u>Hills</u>,
> When <u>all</u> at <u>once</u> I <u>saw</u> a <u>crowd</u>
> A <u>host</u> of <u>dancing</u>[1] <u>Daffodils</u>;

Which has the same sort of feel as:

> She <u>walks</u> in <u>beauty</u>, <u>like</u> the <u>night</u>
> Of <u>cloud</u>less <u>climes</u> and <u>starry</u> <u>skies</u>;
> And <u>all</u> that's <u>best</u> of <u>dark</u> and <u>bright</u>
> Meet <u>in</u> her <u>aspect</u> <u>and</u> her <u>eyes</u>:

---

[1] This is the 1807 version. Wordsworth changed 'dancing' to 'golden' for the 1815 version.

It's beautiful and melancholy and loving. One thing about it, though, is that it has to rhyme. There's an odd thing about English verse that when you have an even number of feet in a line, it doesn't seem right to pause. When you have an odd number of feet, people just naturally take a breath at the end of the line. Why this should be is a complete mystery, but it's almost always true. Try reading this aloud:

> I wandered like a cloud
> That floats o'er vales and hills
> And then I saw a crowd,
> A host of daffodils.

Do you hear how you're pausing? If you try tapping your finger along to the beat, you'll find that the little pause at the end of the line is exactly one beat long. It's as though you're filling in the missing time and making it up to the nearest even number.

The important thing here is that there are two ways of marking the end of a line. You can do it with a rhyme, or you can do it with a pause. And in the tetrameter that second option is out the window. So all tetrameters have to rhyme.

> I wandered lonely as a cloud
> That floats on high o'er vales and hills
> When all at once I saw a host
> Of many dancing buttercups.

Is just nonsense. Of course you can rhyme it in different ways. These ones have been alternating, but you can do the straight couplet, which makes the tetrameter a lot jauntier:

The grave's a fine and private place
But none, I think, do there embrace.

Or you can go the other way entirely and write in the most beautiful and most melancholy form of tetrameter: the *In Memoriam* stanza. Alfred Tennyson's best friend went on holiday and died. This was a bad thing for Tennyson, but a good thing for English poetry, because Tennyson settled down to write 133 short poems about his dead chum, or one long poem in 133 sections, if you want to look at it like that. The entire thing was in iambic tetrameters and they all rhyme the same way:

Dark house, by which once more I stand
Here in the long unlovely street,
Doors, where my heart was used to beat
So quickly, waiting for a hand,

'And eet eet and.' What's so lovely about this is that it takes four lines for the whole thing to make structural sense. If you write in couplets, it's all over in two lines. If you write in alternating rhyme, you're wrapping up after three. But with the *In Memoriam* stanza that first line doesn't make poetic sense until you come to the last syllable of the fourth. It holds and holds, and then completes. So it's rather unfortunate that the most famous lines from the whole poem are usually quoted out of context:

I hold it true, whate'er befall;
I feel it when I sorrow most;
'Tis better to have loved and lost
Than never to have loved at all.

Perhaps we should pause here a moment. Perhaps you think that I'm going on about verse too much. Perhaps you think the stresses don't matter. So to show you that what I'm saying is half true, let's go back and rewrite that in anapaests.

> So I <u>know</u> it is <u>true</u> that <u>what</u>ever be<u>fall;</u>
> And I <u>feel</u> it when<u>ev</u>er I <u>sor</u>row the <u>most;</u>
> That 'tis <u>bet</u>ter to <u>tru</u>ly have <u>loved</u> and have <u>lost</u>
> Than <u>nev</u>er to <u>tru</u>ly have <u>loved</u> one at <u>all</u>.

Quite aside from some little changes in meaning, you can hear how the anapaest changes the feel of the verse. You can also see how easy it is to write verse. It's so easy to throw in a syllable here and there to make up the rhythm. That's why poets are so fond of words like 'Oh' or 'and'. It's not that they keep saying the word in real life, it's just that you can throw it in anywhere. 'And <u>thou</u> art <u>dead</u>, as <u>young</u> and <u>fair</u>'. It's not that Byron usually started sentences with 'and', he just knew the quickest way to make an iambic tetrameter. If you're really stuck you can just repeat a word: 'My <u>love</u> is <u>like</u> a <u>red</u>, red <u>rose</u>'. Or, if you need to lose a syllable, you can do what Tennyson did above and change *whatever* to *whate'er*. The really cheap method is to add an 'a-' to the beginning of a word. The syllables, they are a-changeable.

The Renaissance poet Ben Jonson said that when he wanted to write poetry, he just wrote prose and then mucked around with the word order and banged it with a verbal hammer until it fitted nicely into a verse form. Or:

Ben Jonson in Renaissance claimed
That when a verse to write he aimed [word order mangled
   for rhyme]
He wrote the whole thing down in prose;
And when a meter problem rose, [*arose* wouldn't fit]
He banged it with a verbal hammer,
With clever cut or stammer-stammer,
Until it fitted into verse [*Until* because *till* wouldn't work]
And reckoned it was none the worse.

But Ben Jonson usually wrote in the king of English verse forms, the iambic pentameter.

The iambic pentameter is the Rolls-Royce of verse forms. The others are mere unicycles, tractors, quad-bikes and rickshaws. They're fine for some particular purpose, but the iambic pentameter can do everything. It can do tragic ('No <u>long</u>er <u>mourn</u> for <u>me</u> when <u>I</u> am <u>dead</u>'), heroic ('Once <u>more</u> un<u>to</u> the <u>breach</u>, dear <u>friends</u>, once <u>more</u>'), motivational ('We <u>few</u>, we <u>happy</u> <u>few</u>, we <u>band</u> of <u>broth</u>ers'), pastoral ('There <u>is</u> a <u>will</u>ow <u>grows</u> as<u>lant</u> a <u>brook</u>'), romantic ('If <u>music</u> <u>be</u> the <u>food</u> of <u>love</u>, play <u>on</u>'), casual ('The <u>lady</u> <u>doth</u> pro<u>test</u> too <u>much</u>, me<u>thinks</u>'), or witty:

True <u>wit</u> is <u>na</u>ture <u>to</u> ad<u>van</u>tage <u>dressed</u>,
What <u>oft</u> was <u>thought</u>, but <u>ne'er</u> so <u>well</u> ex<u>pressed</u>.

Shakespeare almost never used another verse form. He didn't need to. It was the iambic pentameter or it was plain prose. Because the pentameter has an odd number of feet, it doesn't need to rhyme. So Shakespeare could write conversations in it that sounded natural and normal. Yet still it always had that subtle beat tapping away underneath. It had a rhythm. Shakespeare could even cut up a pentameter and give each actor half. So Antony says to Cleopatra: 'Com<u>mand</u> me!'

And Cleopatra replies: '<u>O</u>, my <u>par</u>don!'

And Antony replies: '<u>Now</u> I <u>must</u>'.

And you stack 'em all together and get 'Com<u>mand</u> me! <u>O</u>, my <u>par</u>don! <u>Now</u> I <u>must</u>'. So the conversation can keep going without Shakespeare ever breaking the rhythm. The rhythm would get broken after a while, though. In general, Shakespeare has his heroes and his aristocrats natter away in iambic pentameters, but whenever the working classes come on stage they are forced to love, laugh and die in prose, because they're common.

Shakespeare did write one play entirely in prose, but if you've ever seen or read *The Life and Death of King John*, you have my condolences.[2] Like all truly beautiful things, and people, the iambic pentameter gets boring after a while. That's why the prose peasants are such a welcome relief. But on the smaller scale you break it up with variations. Just like the drum fill in the middle of a song, you can have a deliberate metrical break, just for the fun of it. Indeed, there are standard ways to do it. First, you can always add an extra syllable on the end:

To <u>be</u>, or <u>not</u> to <u>be</u>: that <u>is</u> the <u>ques</u>tion:

---

[2] To be fair, *King John* has one of the best speeches in Shakespeare. It's just not worth reading the rest of the play to get there. Act III, scene iii. You're welcome.

The soft syllable simply slides into the pause at the end of the line. The other standard trick is to replace one of the iambs with a trochee, usually the first:

Eyeless in Gaza at the mill with slaves.

Or you can do both:

Whether 'tis nobler in the mind to suffer

But you can put the trochee anywhere really, especially if you're trying to sound all cracked and emotional. You just have to remember to get back in the rhythm afterwards.

For God's | sake, let | us sit upon the ground
And tell sad stories of the death of kings.

When he was in his twenties, Shakespeare was very careful about his pentameters. A little trochee here and there; an extra syllable there. By the time he was in his forties, he'd relaxed and would shuffle things around all the time. He even occasionally added an extra iamb onto the end of the line. That's the sort of wild-man, Devil-may-care versifier he was. But generally, his was a lifelong love affair with the iambic pentameter and almost all his most famous lines, from Romeo to Prospero, from nights Twelfth to Midsummer, go te-TUM te-TUM te-TUM te-TUM te-TUM.

Shakespeare didn't invent the iambic pentameter. It had been the English standard ever since Geoffrey Chaucer began his crafty rhyming in the fourteenth century. Shakespeare simply leapt on a bandwagon and took charge. The iambic pentameter is the most natural form of English. It's how the English language wants to be. And, in all seriousness, I didn't even notice that that last sentence was one until I had typed it.[3]

The iambic pentameter remained the gold standard of English poetry. It's reckoned that about three quarters of all English poetry is written in the meter. Milton used it for *Paradise Lost*. Pope used it for *The Rape of the Lock*. Wordsworth used it for *The Prelude*. Byron used it for *Don Juan*. And ... well ... everybody used it. Half the great lines you know are iambic pentameters.

> Procrastination is the thief of time (Edward Young, 1742)
> They also serve who only stand and wait. (John Milton, 1655)
> To err is human, to forgive divine. (Alexander Pope, 1711)

That last being an example of zeugma.

---

[3] At time of writing, there is a computer program called Pentametron that trawls Twitter looking for anyone who has accidentally written a perfect iambic pentameter. It then looks for another one that rhymes, and thus creates an unending, metrically perfect poem in rhyming couplets.

Chapter 22

⊸∞⊷

Zeugma

Zeugma (pronounced ZOOGmuh) is a funny little rhetorical figure that doesn't work awfully well in English. Still, we might as well cover it. Other figures have produced loads of great lines; it some.

Sometimes you have a series of clauses that all have the same verb. *Tom likes whisky, Dick likes vodka, Harry likes crack cocaine.* That's three *likes*, but you only need one. *Tom likes whisky, Dick vodka, Harry crack cocaine.* The sentence still makes sense, because we understand that that first *likes* is still kind of hanging around in the next few clauses.

With that in mind, let us turn to the most sexist and beautiful lines ever written in English: John Milton in *Paradise Lost* describing the essential differences between chaps and chapesses.

> For contemplation he and valour **formed**,
> For softness she and sweet attractive grace;
> He for God only, she for God in him.

Formed, like one of those upmarket lavatory cleaners, keeps working, even after the flush. Strangely, though, Milton's sentence works. It feels natural in a way that a lot of zeugmas don't. Shakespeare uses the device lots and it always has something of a weird flavour. So Juliet and Romeo run into a little family dispute, 'But passion **lends** them power, time means, to meet'. Of course, time is *lending* them means, but it takes a little moment to work that out. And 'How Tarquin wronged me, I Collatine' sounds just plain wrong in English. If Shakespeare has trouble with a trick, you know it's hard.

Zeugma does have its moments. It makes things sound crisp and clear. You start with a full and florid sentence and then you're down to a bunch of nouns. The first clause sounds normal, the second curt. Zeugma's for the kind of taciturn guy who doesn't waste time on main verbs, or breath on you.

So it works very well occasionally, but only if you want to sound dismissive, as Oscar Wilde did when he said: 'The good end happily and the bad unhappily. That is what fiction means.' It's also what Tennyson used when he had Ulysses dismiss his son's entire life with the words 'He works his work; I mine.'

If a very strict grammarian were listening to Ulysses, he might point out that 'He works his work; I **works** mine' is grammatically all wrong. But it takes a very odd kind of mind to notice that sort of thing.[1] When Othello is told that his wife 'has deceived a father, and may thee', the meaning is obvious and nobody would pick up the error without a notepad and too much spare time.

Usually, zeugma has the verb actually printed in the first clause and then understood in the second (prozeugma). But you can do it the other way around and have the verb in the last clause (hypozeugma). It's even weirder in English, because

---

[1] Very, very, very technically, some scholars (but not all) say that it's zeugma only when it's grammatically wrong. But that applies more to Latin than English.

English is a nice, sequential language where things happen in a sensible order, unlike Latin. But it can be carried off. Shakespeare managed it well once. 'As you on him, Demetrius dote on you.' But that's hardly his greatest line.

There are two reasons that zeugma doesn't really work in English. First, we're not used to seeing verbs miles away from their nouns. The Romans were, and they loved it in a way that makes schoolchildren despair. We can just about manage it here and there, but it's a shock. The second reason is that we would much rather balance clauses in an isocolon (q.v.). 'My true love hath my heart and I have his' wouldn't be nearly as beautiful if it were 'My true love hath my heart, I his', or even 'My true love my heart, I have his', which is, frankly, gibberish.

Poor zeugma! So elegant in the classical world! So silly in ours! Like a toga.

There are a few really famous phrases that use zeugma. It's just that you don't know them. The best measure of a rhetorical figure is how it survives or dies in the popular memory. So some tricks, like diacope, are remembered even when they didn't happen (see Chapter 12); zeugma isn't even when it did.

In 1697 a tragedy by William Congreve was all, or at least most of the rage in London. It was called *The Mourning Bride* and opened with the line 'Music hath charms to soothe the savage breast'. It doesn't quite keep up that standard, but it's really Not Too Bad.

There's a character in *The Mourning Bride* called Zara who's a bit of a bunny-boiler. She's in love with Osmyn, and doesn't realise that not only is Osmyn secretly married to a princess, but that he's not called Osmyn at all. Anyway, she discovers that he and the princess are all sighs and cuddles and decides to work their downfall, or more precisely to have Osmyn (not his real name) executed. She tells him in his prison cell:

> Vile and ingrate! too late thou shalt repent
> The base injustice thou hast done my love:
> Yes, thou shalt know, spite of thy past distress,
> And all those ills which thou so long hast mourned;
> Heav'n has no rage, like love to hatred turned,
> Nor hell a fury, like a woman scorned.

The line is immortal, but not as a zeugma. We chuck a *hath* straight back in ('hell hath no fury, like a woman scorned'), because the popular memory cannot abide the elision. Congreve was probably rather proud of writing the line, but then, as it saith in the Bible, 'pride goeth before destruction and a haughty spirit before a fall'; universally remembered as 'pride goes before a fall'.

Zeugma is a weak figure: good for expressing contempt, and contemptible in other expressions. Can it be improved? 'Can the Ethiopian change his skin, or the leopard his spots?' (Jeremiah 13, verse 23)

So the memorable phrases that employed zeugma prove that zeugma isn't memorable. This is a paradox.

Chapter 23

―∞―

Paradox

Paradoxes are remarkably hard to define, but you know one when you see one. Mathematicians, logicians, psychologists, sociologists and poets all compete for the word. They all think they own it. But this is untrue. For paradoxes are quite paradoxical.

Let's start with Oscar Wilde, master of inversion. Most of Wilde's paradoxes are not paradoxes at all. They are simply simple thoughts expressed in a terribly surprising way.

> In this world there are only two tragedies. One is not getting what one wants, and the other is getting it.
> – Oscar Wilde, *Lady Windermere's Fan*, 1892

> There are two tragedies in life. One is to lose your heart's desire. The other is to gain it.
> – George Bernard Shaw, *Man and Superman*, 1903

Really, there's no paradox here. You or I might have said 'screwed either way', but not Wilde. He simply sets the sentence up as though it's going to mention two separate things, and then doubles back on himself. The content is not paradoxical. The phrasing is. And as a result the audience are just as pleased as they would have been if Wilde had invented a real paradox. It is style not substance that counts, and the superficial qualities that last, even when the deeper nature has been found out.

Exactly the same thing goes with:

> There is only one thing in the world worse than being talked
> about, and that is not being talked about.

It's not a paradox, but a statement of grumpy resignation. But
it is phrased like a paradox. To borrow a term from logic, it is a
veridical paradox, one that only appears impossible, but is in fact
quite simple. Wilde pushes this trick a little further with:

> All women become like their mothers. That is their tragedy. No
> man does, and that is his.

This could have been phrased, 'Why is it that your girlfriend's
mother is always annoying, but your male friends' mothers are
always lovely?' But instead, it was phrased as a veridical paradox.
Wilde does do real paradoxes, but I'll come to them when I've
dealt with puns.

The pun-paradox is, perhaps, the runt of the litter. It is at
the same time a paradox and merely a pun. Both and neither.
When Crystal Gayle sang 'Don't It Make My Brown Eyes Blue'
she was, at the same time, contradicting Wittgenstein's axiom
that no part of the visual field can simultaneously be of two
hues, and making a statement that anybody familiar with the
English language will find unexceptionable, as unexceptionable
as John Lennon's assertion that red was the colour that would
make him blue or his complaint that he was both black and
blue. British politics was altered by such a paradox with the most
famous poster in electoral history: a queue of people snaking
away into the distance, and the slogan 'Labour Isn't Working'.

The people in the queue were all actually very well-employed, at Conservative Central Office, but the paradox was perfect. Politics is full of potential for such things, but for some reason nobody has used the slogan 'The Left is Right', or 'The Right is Wrong' (aside from the Johnny Cash song 'The One on the Right Is on the Left'). The punning paradox is, perhaps, no paradox at all, but it is intriguing and it is memorable, and *Back to the Future* made a tidy profit.

But the pun leads us closer to the true paradox, because it at least looks like one. When Oscar Wilde said that 'We live in an age when unnecessary things are our only necessities' he was still being veridical, but he was heading towards the central contradiction. Luxury is, for the human, a necessity; what are commonly called the necessities can usually be dispensed with. Chance is a certainty and living is only the slow process of dying. And here we find ourselves pushing towards the 'what it's all about', but only pushing so far. Even Shakespeare saying 'I must be cruel only to be kind' didn't push his foot over the threshold. Wilde never clasped the full and fascinating contradiction, he never said anything that didn't make sense, or make you laugh, after a few moments' thought. He would do anything for a good paradox, but he wouldn't do that.

The true paradox is one of the more peculiar points of rhetoric in its long war against reality. We will happily dream the impossible dream, even if logic and the laws of the universe say that it's … impossible. The true paradox is arresting because it breaks all laws, but calming because that is so easy in language. It is easy to write that black is white, that up is down and that good is evil. It's as easy as typing, and as difficult. I can't do it, and I just did.

But by breaking the laws of the universe, the true paradox lifts us out of it. The true paradox is, necessarily, a mystical moment, despite the fact that from a writer's point of view it's immensely easy. My fingers need only tap the keyboard for every cop to be a criminal and all the sinners saints. But the reader can meditate on the words for ever.

It is easy, therefore, to see the true paradox as being false; as being an easy trick and therefore worthless. It is an easy trick, but it is in no way worthless. A well executed paradox stirs the soul and mixes language and philosophy in a way that no other figure does. Paul Simon was on to something when he titled his song 'The Sound of Silence', and his verse about people talking without speaking, and about people hearing without listening, was easy for him, but that makes it no less beautiful to us.

The paradox is most at home in religion. Before Abraham was, I am. God's service is perfect freedom. He is a circle whose centre is everywhere and whose circumference is nowhere. These ideas may not be geometrically workable from an engineering point of view, but the ideas that they stir are of thought outside mere reality, and by their very operation on the human mind, they show themselves to have value, because such operation is itself proof, to have such thoughts is to prove that such thoughts can exist. And though that may not matter, it does.

So it is no surprise to us to hear paradoxes from the mouth of a mystic. We hear the words 'The first shall be last, and the last shall be first' and we *react* in a mystical way. Or at least, most chaps do; for myself I just consider it a good example of chiasmus.

Chapter 24

Chiasmus

Human beings, for some reason or another, like symmetry. You leave a bunch of them next to a jungle for a couple of days and you'll come back to find an ornamental garden. We take stones and turn them into the Taj Mahal or St Paul's Cathedral. Of course, a few things in nature are symmetrical anyway – snowflakes and leaves and the like – but their symmetry is never at a glance; you have to hold the leaf up at the right angle or run through the blizzard with a magnifying glass. When a chap makes something symmetrical he tends to set up a grand avenue so that you can see it is, and then he puts trees on either side. Nature is not symmetrical and symmetry is not natural.

This love of symmetry carries straight over into words. At the smallest level you have the palindrome where the letters answer one another across the sentence. The palindrome is an old tradition: the first thing that man ever said was, probably, 'Madam, I'm Adam'. And it has caused terrible distress to even the greatest literary minds. The only reason that T.S. Eliot insisted on the middle initial was that he was painfully aware of what his name would have been without it, backwards. For a short while, he became so paranoid that he decided to use his middle name instead and introduced himself as T. Stearns Eliot. The phase did not last, but it's probably why his first great poem was called 'The Love Song of J. Alfred Prufrock'.

But beyond the microscopic symmetries of the palindrome there are the grander and more obvious ones of chiasmus, where the words of the first half are mirrored in the second. There was a musical that came out in 1925 called *No, No, Nanette*. But the only lines anybody can remember now are:

Tea for two and two for tea
Me for you and you for me

There's something lovely about the symmetry here, not because it's visual like a palindrome, but because the thoughts replicate each other. 'Me for you' is mirrored, requited and answered by 'you for me'. Also everybody likes a cup of tea now and then. Requited love is only a pleasing symmetry, and symmetry is a kind of justice. The Three Musketeers had a cry of 'All for one and one for all'. The symmetry makes it memorable but also reflects the reciprocity. It is that great human symmetry: the deal.

Socrates may or may not have said, 'Eat to live, not live to eat'. We remember the line because the two thoughts are held up as in a mirror: one reversing the other. It also, I suspect, reflects the fact that the Ancient Greek diet involved a lot of porridge.

Mind you, just reversing words is almost as hard as a palindrome. It gets you stuck. Stuck. You get it? Thus writers can allow themselves a little give, a little wiggle-room, a little loosening of the literary belt. For example, a contemporary American writer with the peculiar name of Snoop Doggy Dogg (God, God poons) wrote a confessional poem about having 'my mind on my money and my money on my mind'. While another, more financially optimistic chap called Tupac (Caput) observed jovially that 'money don't make the man, but man I'm making money'.

Americans seem particularly fond of such verbal symmetries, and tend to elect anybody who can come up with a symmetrical sentence. The current President told his troops: 'You stood up for America, now America must stand up for you.' The one before didn't care 'whether we bring our enemies to justice, or bring justice to our enemies'. Before that it was: 'People the world over have always been more impressed by the power of our example than by the example of our power', and so on and so forth.

Even those who have never made it to President have given chiasmus a go because their chances are gone without chiasmus. Mitt Romney tried 'Freedom requires religion, just as religion requires freedom', and Hillary Clinton tried for the White House with: 'In the end, the true test is not the speeches a president delivers, it's whether the president delivers on the speeches.'

All of this goes back to JFK's inauguration speech, which was chiasmus-crazy. With the Cold War at its coldest, Kennedy told America that 'Mankind must put an end to war, or war will put an end to mankind'. His method was peaceful: 'Let us never negotiate out of fear, but let us never fear to negotiate.' And most famously of all he told Americans: 'Ask not what your country can do for you, but what you can do for your country.'

Kennedy started the craze for chiasmus in American politics, but he himself had probably got the idea from his father. Joseph Kennedy, quite aside from being a businessman, diplomat and politician, is the prime suspect for originating the phrase later immortalised by Billy Ocean: 'When the going gets tough, the tough get going.'

Chiasmus always sounds the same – the carefully thought-out artificial symmetry – but it can take various forms. First of all, there's the straight repetition, of which Edward Lear was so fond:

They went to sea in a Sieve, they did,
In a Sieve they went to sea:

Or:

Oh, lovely Pussy, oh, Pussy, my love,
What a beautiful Pussy you are …

The cat sat on the mat, and on the mat sat the cat. This form of chiasmus is just repetition in a mirror. It's easy to do, and to do it is easy. Chiasmus really comes into its own when the inversion of the words gives you an inversion of thought as well. JFK's great chiasmus works because *you* and *your country* are swapped around. The doer becomes the done for and the done for becomes the doer. It's the same idea that Jesus used with 'The Sabbath was made for man and not man for the Sabbath' or 'Judge not, that ye be not judged'.

Here the thoughts seem to be symmetrical, and thus they somehow seem to be logical as well. The sentence has the air of a clear, well-thought-out argument. The world makes sense in a chiasmus like this. The rational, or at least symmetrical, mind of man has a place for everything, and everything in its place. As Keats put it, 'Beauty is truth, truth beauty'. Or as Edward Fitzgerald said: 'The moving finger writes; and, having writ; / Moves on.'

The repetition and logic come together in the chiasmus of the Venn diagram. Byron pointed out that 'Pleasure's a sin, and sometimes sin's a pleasure', which I suppose was a subject on which he was the expert. Oscar Wilde said that 'All crime is vulgar, just as all vulgarity is crime', and then got sent off to Reading Gaol to reconsider and write ballads. Both these lines use chiasmus to get around one of the problems of precise logic: if all tomatoes are red, does that mean that all red things are tomatoes? Chiasmus lets you explain, and sound rather elegant while you're doing so.

Chiasmus can also be used for something very like a pun. Mae West said, 'It's not the men in my life, it's the life in my men', where *life* is being used in two different senses (CV vs. vigour). Dorothy Parker allegedly went one further. The story (unconfirmed) goes that her editor at *The New Yorker* sent a telegram to Parker while she was on her honeymoon. The editor wanted to remind her about the deadline for an article she was meant to be writing. Dorothy Parker sent one back saying: 'I've been too fucking busy, and vice versa.' This seems remarkably unlikely, as you couldn't normally send swear words in a telegram, which of course had to be dictated to the chap at the post office. So maybe another version of the tale is true, where a colleague complained of being too fucking busy, and Parker merely murmured, 'Or vice versa'. Or maybe it was all made up. It is, nonetheless, a rare case of chiasmus implied, but not stated.

One of the things that makes Dorothy Parker's chiasmus a trifle unlikely is that a good chiasmus needs to be thought out. Chiasmus is clever, but not natural. Kennedy's inauguration speech could never have been improvised and Mae West, one suspects, took a while to work hers out. Chiasmus is the grand statement, it's the victory of symmetry, it's the Taj Mahal. There is, though, a more subtle form: the grammatical chiasmus.

Adjective noun : noun adjective, or as Milton put it in the closing line of *Lycidas*: 'Tomorrow to fresh woods and pastures new.' It's a bit of a wrench to move that 'new' to the end, but it completes a symmetry. More accomplished is the opening line 'I see trees of green, red roses too' from 'What a Wonderful World',[1] where the sentence is *plant colour : colour plant*. An unwary chap may sing that line all day without noticing the chiasmus.

It is possible, just possible, to make things symmetrical without anybody really noticing. They still like what they hear, but they're not sure why. Here, the grand oratory of Kennedy or the ingenuity of Mae West are gone, and in their place are the gentle symmetries of Dr Johnson. Johnson wrote in *The Vanity of Human Wishes* about the world of pleasure-seekers who indulged in 'By day the frolic, and the dance by night', which sounds rather agreeable, not just because a schedule of 24-hour dancing and frolicking is a good schedule, but because the sentence runs *time activity : activity time*.

Coleridge did the same subtle thing in 'Kubla Khan' when he dreamt of his 'sunny pleasure-dome with caves of ice'. But that poem also contains the rarest, subtlest, strangest kind of chiasmus there is. It's a species of chiasmus that is as hard to spot in the wild as the Abominable Snowman, and therefore as hard to study, and it occurs in the great opening line:

In Xanadu did Kubla Khan …

---

[1] By Bob Thiele and George David Weiss, released 1967.

Did you see it? Look again. Nothing? It's not a symmetry of grammar, or words being mirrored; yet there is a reason why that line rolls off the tongue like the milk of paradise. Give up?

An – Ah – Oo – i – Oo – Ah – An
In Xanadu did Kubla Khan

It's a chiasmus of vowels. Tennyson wrote:

Beneath the thunders of the upper deep
Ee – e – u – e – o – e – u – e – ee

A symmetry of assonance.

Chapter 25

———— ⚭ ————

Assonance

Assonance is repeating a vowel sound: *deep heat* or *blue moon*. It is, I'm afraid, the thin and flimsy cousin of alliteration. Well, it is in English. Welsh poetry, I'm told, thrives on assonance, as did Old German and Hebrew. But in English it's hard to tell whether it's there at all. There are probably a few reasons for this. First of all, English doesn't use many vowels.

Half the vowels in English aren't what you thought they were. They're *schwas*. A proper vowel is formed in a particular part of the mouth. So E is near the front, I is at the top, and Ooo is at the back. A schwa is formed in the middle. It sounds a bit like all the vowels, and is really none of them. It's a lazy compromise between all the proper vowels, and we use it all the time. The word *another* may be spelt An-Oth-Er but you pronounce it uh-nuh-thuh. You may pronounce the *bout* in *about* clearly, but what's the first vowel? It's a schwa. Uh-bout.

There's even a letter for this grunty, nothing sound: ə. If you start using this lettə you get an ideə of how ubiquətəs schwa is. It's the most commən vowəl in English – not A or E or any of the vowəls you learnt at school, but schwa. Not ə lot of peopəl know that.

The importance of all this for assonance is that English is missing a bunch of its vowels, or at least uses a vague, half-arsed compromise vowel that sounds like all and none. There is a second problem, though. Vowels change.

Over the centuries and over the classes, consonants tend to stay roughly the same, while vowels slip around like eels. As long as the consonant is there, the word is still recognisable. A middle-class Englishman *ate* lunch, the Queen *et* lunch, and a Cockney street urchin *ite* it. So nobody is utterly sure how Shakespeare pronounced his vowels. Shakespeare makes a habit of rhyming *love* with *prove*. That may be because Shakespeare pronounced *prove* as *pruv*, or it might just be that Shakespeare pronounce *love* as *luve*. If he did, then 'If music be the food of love, play on' has an awful lot of assonance in it: *muse, fude, luve*. But as Shakespeare didn't have a tape-recorder we'll never know. The point for this chapter is, I'm afraid, that Shakespeare's works may have been filled with lovely assonances that are now lost for ever. 'Is this' has assonance on 'i'. 'A dagger that' has assonance on 'a'. 'I see before me' has assonance on 'ee'. But it might not have done in the original.

And even in the cases where you can find it, it's hard to be certain that it's anything more than a coincidence. There are only so many vowel sounds. It's terribly tempting to look at Tennyson's great line

To strive, to seek, to find, and not to yield

... and say 'Golly, it's four verbs that go *i ee i ee*.' But that might be a coincidence. Did Auden write 'Stop all the clocks' because he liked the assonance of 'o', or because he was writing about ... well ... stopping clocks? When Dylan Thomas raged against the *dying* of the *light*, perhaps he just didn't want the light to die. The only phrase where I'd say with some certainty that assonance made it famous is:

I met a traveller from an antique land

Three *ans* in a row, with the very odd word 'antique' evidence of how deliberate it is. But that, after much searching, is my best candidate. It's not like alliteration.

The one place that you can be sure that a little bit of assonance has been important is in proverbs and phrases. Why are you as high as a kite and not a cloud? Why as happy as Larry and not Peter? How now, brown cow?

The only reason that a stitch in time saves nine is the assonance. If it saved eight the phrase would be forgotten. English cats have nine lives, in Germany they have *sechs Leben*. You may, of course, be wondering why either of these phrases needed a particular number; that's all down to the Fourteenth Rule.

Chapter 26

—⚬⚬⚬—

The Fourteenth Rule[1]

Some people think that the number thirteen is unlucky. Why they should think this is utterly unclear. All sorts of explanations get offered – thirteen people at the Last Supper, thirteen steps to the gallows – but they all look like nonsense. You might as well believe that seven is lucky or that the answer to the question of life, the universe and everything is 42.

The idea that a number can have some sort of special significance is called numerology. And there are as many systems of numerology as there have been cultures, periods of history, and plonkers to think them up. Well, to be fair they weren't all plonkers. Pythagoras was a clever chap but he still mucked around with numerology and believed that odd numbers were masculine and even feminine. But I don't think you need to be too much of a spoilsport sceptic to suspect that numerology is nonsense.

The fact that something that's so obviously nonsense is so popular shows that it must appeal to something deep, deep within us. That the West thinks that seven is lucky and the Chinese think eight is shows both that numerology is wrong and that it's popular across the world. Numbers feel mysterious and significant. So all you need to do to sound mysterious and significant is to pick a number, any number.

---

[1] This is the only rule I'm including that is not part of classical rhetoric.

You would have to have a heart of stone and a soul of Formica to listen to 'A Whiter Shade of Pale' without wondering to yourself why there are sixteen vestal virgins. What? What does the number mean? Why sixteen? What's the reason? There is, of course, no reason and the truth is plain to see: it *feels* so mysterious. If she had been one of several vestal virgins, the song would be Much Less Memorable.

Folk songs and fairy tales are bursting with such strangely significant numbers. It has to be four-and-twenty blackbirds baked in the pie, and three blind mice, and fifteen men on a dead man's chest because if you replace those numbers with 'several' or 'a lot of' the whole feeling is lost – the feeling of significance, of something ancient and mysterious.

Coleridge knew all about the power of numbers. *The Rime of the Ancient Mariner* is a classic example. It's almost an exercise in enumeration. He starts it off in the second line:

It is an ancient Mariner,
And he stoppeth one of three.

Why three? Perhaps it represents the Christian trinity? Or perhaps there's no particular point to the number. And Coleridge doesn't stop there. There aren't just lots of people on the ship, there are:

Four times fifty living men

… who are condemned when a pale lady 'whistles thrice'. Things don't happen in weeks, they happen in:

Seven days, seven nights, I saw that curse,
And yet I could not die.

Like one that hath been seven days drowned
My body lay afloat;

The albatross accompanies the ship for precisely nine days, and the spirit follows the boat not 'deep in the sea', as most poets would have put it, but exactly 'nine fathoms deep'.

A hundred and one other authors have used the trick: Tolkien's Nine Ring Wraiths and Lawrence of Arabia's Seven Pillars of Wisdom.[2] As Rudyard Kipling observed:

… my Totem saw the shame; from his ridgepole shrine
  he came,
And he told me in a vision of the night:—
'There are nine and sixty ways of constructing tribal lays,
And every single one of them is right!'

But the most prolific enumerator is almost certainly Bob Dylan. Bob Dylan writes folk songs and there is something inescapably folky about numbers. He puts numbers everywhere: sad forests (seven), wild horses (six), jugglers (fifteen), believers (five) and fourth time around. There are at least 573 other examples, including 'Love Minus Zero', which is an example of catachresis.

---

[2] This is taken from the Bible, Proverbs 9, verse 1, but the point remains.

Chapter 27

---∞∞∞---

Catachresis

Catachresis is rather difficult to define, but it's essentially when a sentence is so startlingly wrong that it's right. Catachresis is the slap in the face. It's the ice-block in your underwear. Catachresis is bam! Unfortunately, the most famous example is barely noticeable.

Even the bravest of chaps can have a loss of nerve when faced with the harrowing and fearful task of chatting to his mother. A dutiful son has to remember not to slouch or swear or, in Hamlet's case, murder the old bat. So he gives himself a pep talk full of reminders:

> … now to my mother.
> O heart, lose not thy nature; let not ever
> The soul of Nero enter this firm bosom:
> Let me be cruel, not unnatural:
> I will speak daggers to her, but use none.

Nero was notorious for putting his own mother to death, among other indiscretions, and Hamlet's words would make a wonderful Mother's Day card. Yet the important phrase here is the catachresis 'I will speak daggers'. If you stop and think about it, the sentence doesn't make sense. You can't speak a dagger.[1]

---

[1] Shakespeare was reusing a trick he'd first tried in *Much Ado About Nothing* where Benedick says that Beatrice 'speaks poinards, and every word stabs'.

You can speak any adverb. You can speak loudly, softly, gradually, democratically and deliciously. You can speak a few nouns: English and the truth. Or you could speak words as sharp as daggers, or as cruel. But you can't *speak daggers* any more than you can speak grenades or bullets or blunderbusses. And that's why the phrase stuck. Speaking daggers is so unusual that it became part of the language. And then it became usual. And a couple of hundred years later we got *looking daggers* (1834) and nobody really notices any more. It's the fate of everyone who sets out to shock: you shock, you are noticed, you are remembered, but what is remembered ceases to be noticed and shocks no more. *Sic transit l'enfant terrible d'antan.*

The same thing happened to Lewis Carroll and his great catachresis. Alice drinks the drink that says 'Drink Me' and it makes her small. Then she eats the cake that says 'Eat Me' and it makes her big. And then:

> 'Curiouser and curiouser!' cried Alice (she was so much surprised, that for the moment she quite forgot how to speak good English).

But the *Oxford English Dictionary* now has an entry of its own just for *curiouser and curiouser* (meaning 16 C under 'curious'), with Carroll as the first citation.

But catachresis continues in a cycle of novelty and absorption. It is very hard to explain grammatically why it is that 'Thunderbirds are go'. But if Thunderbirds were going it would never have caught on. It's that single word that hits you like first love, and, like a first love, seems rather familiar 40 years later.

Songwriters love to use love as a catachresis. For example, there's Leonard Cohen's 'Dance Me to the End of Love'. That's a perfect catachresis. You would expect the sentence to end with a noun of space or time – 'Dance Me to the End of the Night' or 'Dance Me to the End of the Street' – and instead you get love, which isn't a place, unless you believe The Doors' line 'She lives on Love Street', which is another love-catachresis. Bananarama had 'Love in the First Degree', Moon Martin had a 'Bad Case of Loving You', and KLF had asked 'What Time Is Love?' Rolf Harris attempted his own catachresis with 'Tie Me Kangaroo Down, Sport', but the most beautiful catachresis is probably Roxette's opening line, 'Lay a whisper on my pillow'.

A catachresis is any sentence that makes you stop, scratch your head and say 'that's wrong', before you suddenly realise that it's right. It's Andrew Marvell in 'The Garden':

Annihilating all that's made
To a green thought in a green shade.

Or it's the modern host asking his guest: 'Would you like some I Can't Believe It's Not Butter?'

Although that's also a litotes.

Chapter 28

――― ❧ ―――

Litotes

Litotes is affirming something by denying its opposite. It's not difficult. Supposing you're writing a song about something that happens every day. You could start each line with the words 'It's usual', or you could use litotes and start them with the words 'It's not unusual'. Litotes is a form of understatement-by-negative, and is not without its uses.

Understatement is a tricky business, because it works only if you know the truth. If Franz Liszt told you that he played the piano a little, it would be an understatement. If I said the same it would just be true. So, in a sense, understaters need you to know what they're saying before they say it. Or, at the very least, they need you to get it instantly. 'The Burial of Sir John Moore at Corunna' begins:

> Not a drum was heard, not a funeral note,
> As his corpse to the rampart we hurried.

And the reader has to pick up on the fact that there was silence. A logician might say that it was still possible that there was cheering and heavy traffic and sirens going off, but logicians have no place near poetry. When Tom Jones sees you hanging around with anyone, we know that he cries and cries consistently.

The context is often a help. Antarctic explorers can joke to each other about how it's 'not warm' all day long (and remember

that during exploring season the day is four months at the South
Pole). Or you can refer to something universally acknowledged:
'Bill Gates isn't short of a bob or two.' But even context can let
you down. On 15 August 1945, Emperor Hirohito made a broad-
cast to the Japanese nation. It was the first time an Emperor
had ever spoken on the radio, so the Japanese people knew that
something was up. Moreover, two atomic bombs had just been
dropped. Hirohito announced to his listening nation that 'the
war situation has developed not necessarily to Japan's advan-
tage', which is perhaps the most extreme example of litotes in all
humanity's huge history. But it wasn't quite clear enough. Many
listeners didn't realise what he was saying until the speech was
over and the announcer cut in to say that Japan had surrendered
to the Allies.

Litotes requires you to know your audience, and preferably
have them in the room with you. When the Empress of India
(and Queen of Great Britain and Ireland) tried her litotes she
kept it short-range and brutal.

> Her [Queen Victoria's] remarks can freeze as well as crystallise.
> There is a tale of the unfortunate equerry who ventured dur-
> ing dinner at Windsor to tell a story with a spice of scandal or
> impropriety in it. 'We are not amused,' said the Queen when he
> had finished.

Litotes is a complicated beast. It's closely related to the
double-negative, but it's not quite the same. Leaving no stone
unturned is not litotes, because it has no understatement to
it. When Shakespeare wrote in *The Tempest*, 'I have no hope
that he's undrowned', it wasn't a litotes because it wasn't an

understatement, it was just confusing. Litotes is a special kind of understatement that happens to use negatives. And understatement is a kind of irony.

Irony is an odd fish because, contrary to popular belief, irony draws people together. Irony is an untruth that both parties know is untrue, that both parties agree is untrue.[1] When two strangers meet in the pouring rain and one says to the other, 'Lovely weather we're having', he's appealing to the one thing that he knows they both have in common and the one truth they both recognise. When a couple are arguing furiously and one says sarcastically to the other, 'Oh, because you'd know all about being faithful', they may be arguing, but that statement appeals to knowledge they share.

Irony is always about what people have in common, and so is litotes. It's a sociable figure. Though it can be used to end wars, bury generals and crush courtiers, litotes is most at home among friends. It is a gentlemanly figure, a civilised figure, an agreeable one. It is the sort of figure you should toss out with an amiable smile and a raised eyebrow.

'Well I'll be damned if it isn't old Bertie. How are you?'

'Can't complain, old boy, can't complain.'

'Would it be awfully wrong to tempt you with a drink?'

'I wouldn't say no.'

However, there are those who don't like litotes at all, and they are not without their reasons. George Orwell wrote a long essay attacking hackneyed metaphors and language that wasn't crystal clear – or, as he would have put it, diamond clear. His general theory was that unclear language reflected unclear thought,

---

[1] I'm excluding dramatic, proleptic and situational irony.

which allowed evil politicians to oppress people. So litotes is a dictator's henchman.

Orwell reckoned that 'it should also be possible to laugh the not un- formation out of existence'. He advised all writers to memorise the sentence *A not unblack dog was chasing a not unsmall rabbit across a not ungreen field*. However, writers didn't memorise that sentence and litotes continued untroubled until its reputation was nearly destroyed by the cruel despot John Major.

Hansard, the record of the proceedings of the British Parliament, has absolutely no record of John Major ever saying the words 'not inconsiderable';[2] but it became his catchphrase nonetheless. These days no journalist ever refers to the twentieth century's second longest serving Prime Minister without working the phrase in somewhere. Though he never said it, the litotes seemed to sum up all that the public found wrong in him. Where Thatcher would have said 'big' and Churchill 'vast', Major footled about with a double-negative. Where was the oratory? Where was the charisma? Why didn't he just come out and say 'considerable'? It was a slur, but it was a slur that stuck.

Litotes isn't the best figure to use when you're trying to be grand. Litotes does not stir the soul, it's more suited to stirring tea. Even Wordsworth couldn't make it work like that. He was pretty damned good at raising the spirits and soul, but he had the silly habit of using the phrase 'not seldom'. 'Not seldom, clad in radiant vest, / Deceitfully goes forth the Morn', 'Not seldom

---

[2] I have been unable to find any reference to Major ever actually using these words in any context except once in a 1992 speech where he said: 'It is, of course, as *Private Eye* or the *Guardian* would have me say, a time "of not inconsiderable interest in Europe"'. Of course, it's not easy to prove a negative.

from the uproar I retired', 'Not seldom did we stop to watch some tuft / Of dandelion seed', 'not seldom in my walks / A momentary trance comes over me', and on and on until you want to grab him, slap him, pull out a dictionary and show him the word 'often'.

So Orwell wasn't wrong, but he wasn't quite right either. Litotes has no place in politics or pastoral poetry. Litotes cannot stand on a podium or cry from a mountaintop, it is much more at home in the drawing room or the bathtub. It's the sort of figure that should be used by Bertie Wooster. In fact, it was used by Bertie Wooster:

> As I sat in the bathtub, soaping a meditative foot and singing, if I remember correctly, 'Pale Hands I Loved Beside the Shalimar', it would be deceiving my public to say that I was feeling boomps-a-daisy.[3]

Where 'Pale Hands I Loved Beside the Shalimar' is an example of synecdoche.

---

[3] *Jeeves and the Feudal Spirit* (1954) by P.G. Wodehouse.

Chapter 29

―――⊗⊗⊗―――

Metonymy and Synecdoche

Everybody knows about metaphors and similes; metonym and synecdoche are the exact opposite. In metaphor and simile you say that two things have a couple of qualities in common. It generally has to be at least two: one obvious one and one that is strongly implied. Suppose that a chap tells the girl he loves that her eyes are as green as emeralds: she'll probably take that as a compliment, not because emeralds are green but because they're valuable. If he tells the girl that her eyes are as green as mould, he'll get a slap; not because he's inaccurate but because it's always the second, implied comparison that's important. Green as beer-bottles suggests that she's drunk, and green as traffic-lights will probably get him arrested. 'Your heart is as cold as ice' is completely different to 'Your heart is as cold as ice cream', even though the temperatures are the same.

I wandered lonely as a cloud …

Clouds are not lonely. Especially in the Lake District where Wordsworth wrote that line. In the Lake District clouds are remarkably sociable creatures that bring their friends and relatives and stay for weeks. But nobody even notices that the comparison is all wrong because the mind always skips to the second connection which is that clouds do wander aimlessly.

It's not that Wordsworth didn't know about meteorology, it's that he did know about metaphor.

In the same year that Wordsworth was writing about hiking on English hillsides – 1804 – William Blake was writing a poem about hiking on English hillsides. Blake's poem is a bit different. For starters it's about the medieval legend that Jesus spent his twenties in Britain. There is no evidence for this whatsoever, and, so far as historians can tell, Britain's tourism industry was scandalously underdeveloped at the time. The idea was too ridiculous even for Blake, which is why he hedges his bets and phrases everything as a question. The other difference is that Blake doesn't use metaphor, he uses metonymy, and more precisely synecdoche.

Metaphor is when two things are connected because they are similar, metonymy is when two things are connected because they are really physically connected. It's the favourite rhetorical figure of Fleet Street. Consider the following news report:

> Downing Street was left red-faced last night at news that the White House was planning to attack the British Crown with the support of Wall Street. Number 10 said it was 'unacceptable' though the Vatican refused to get involved. Meanwhile, the army's top brass have been ordered to send in the Green Jackets, which will confuse the Americans as they were expecting the Redcoats.

Rather than mentioning people, you mention something that they are physically touching. You are no longer you. You are your clothes, you are the building you're standing in, the medals pinned to your chest or the hat on your head. You are a suit, a blue-stocking, a bit of skirt.

The extreme form of metonymy is synecdoche, where you become one of your body parts. You are your feet, your lips or your liver.

> All eyes were on the government as they tried to alleviate the famine with a charity theatre matinée. A spokesman said if they got enough bums on seats they could feed all the hungry mouths, but it would have to be all hands on deck as this was about getting feet on the ground. The government said they had their top brains working on it and that the gate from a full house could buy a hundred head of cattle.

So how do you apply that to a poem about Jesus going for stroll?

> And did those feet in ancient time
> Walk upon England's mountains green? […]
> And did the countenance divine
> Shine forth upon our clouded hills?

William Blake loved synecdoche. His poems are filled with stray body-parts.

> What immortal hand or eye
> Could frame thy fearful symmetry?

Or

> And what shoulder and what art
> Could twist the sinews of thy heart?

And when that heart began to beat,
What dread hands and what dread feet?

What makes Blake's synecdoches so powerful is that we get glimpses. It's like the opening of a film where we see just a close-up of feet walking on green grass, a hand or an eye in the night-time forests. But whereas in a film the camera would pull out to show the whole scene, Blake never reveals. We see the feet and the shining countenance, but when he pulls out they've been replaced by a lamb. Blake works in fragments; when you read his synecdoches you have to see the world in a grain of sand.

And synecdoches can be so vivid, that's the power of the close-up. When Dr Faustus sold his soul to the Devil, part of his price was to see the most beautiful woman who had ever lived: Helen of Troy. She was brought before him and he asked:

Was this the face that launched a thousand ships
And burnt the topless towers of Ilium?

He didn't need to phrase it like that. He could have said:

Is this the woman for the sake of whose beauty the Greeks launched a large naval force and besieged the city of Troy (also known as Ilium), a siege that eventually resulted in the city being sacked and burnt?

The meaning would have been exactly the same. But Christopher Marlowe didn't write it like that. He used three synecdoches. Helen is only a face. The Trojan War is a snapshot image of a thousand ships setting sail. Troy is only burning towers.

Ten years of elaborate Greek mythology in three clear images: a face, a flotilla, and turrets set ablaze.

All this relies, of course, on the historical synecdoche, where one part of a story stands for the whole thing, not because it's a symbol of it, but because it's part of it. The Boston Tea Party, the storming of the Bastille, and the fall of the Berlin Wall are all synecdoches. They are fragments that narrate a whole story.

The hand that rocks the cradle rules the world, and the right fragment implies the world. And we are nothing more than hungry eyes, cheating hearts, lying lips, and faithless arms. Although all those are also transferred epithets.

Chapter 30

Transferred Epithets

A transferred epithet is when an adjective is applied to the wrong noun. So instead of writing 'The nervous man smoked a cigarette' you write 'The man smoked a nervous cigarette'. Cigarettes, of course, do not have feelings; yet we understand immediately what that second sentence means. A transferred epithet is a good thing, or, rather, a good epithet is a transferred thing.

It's astonishing how often epithets are transferred and how little we notice. Nobody ever stops to think about a disabled toilet, and why and how it has been disabled. Perhaps the flush has been sabotaged or the U-bend deliberately blocked. Once you point out the transfer, it becomes rather amusing. P.G. Wodehouse was the great master of this technique. His transfers are just a little too ridiculous to work. 'I lit a rather pleased cigarette' is just a bit too much, as is 'I balanced a thoughtful lump of sugar on the teaspoon'; but Wodehouse's best, for my considered money, was: 'His eyes widened and an astonished piece of toast fell from his grasp.'[1] The idea of astonished toast is just too much, and we let out a surprised chortle.

But the transferred epithet is not always fun and games. 'Dulce et Decorum Est' by Wilfred Owen is a pretty grim poem

---

[1] For a fuller analysis see 'The Transferred Epithet in P.G. Wodehouse' by Robert A. Hall, Jr., *Linguistic Inquiry*, Vol. 4, No. 1 (Winter, 1973), pp. 92–4.

about the effects of mustard gas, but the transferred *clumsy* fits right in:

> Gas! Gas! Quick, boys! – An ecstasy of fumbling,
> Fitting the clumsy helmets just in time …

And in Gray's *Elegy* it feels really rather … elegiac:

> The ploughman homeward plods his weary way

We don't laugh at the idea that the way is weary rather than the ploughman. It feels natural, particularly, for some reason, with roads. We accept that miles can be weary, roads lonesome and highways lost, because we know that in each case the adjective describes the weary, lonesome, lost chap and not the thoroughfare.

T.S. Eliot was a compulsive transferrer of epithets. In a mere three lines of 'Prufrock' retreats mutter, nights are restless, hotels are one-night, and restaurants are made of, or possibly serve saw-dust, it isn't clear which. Presumably the saw-dust is on the floor, but one of the odd things about the transferred epithet is that you don't need to even mention the noun that should be taking the adjective. You can leave it to be guessed. You need only mention the dizzy heights and imagination will supply the human.

Epithets are almost always transferred between humans and their surroundings, and it's almost always a one-way street. The emotions leak out from us. The loneliness seeps through the soles of our shoes onto the road. Our clumsiness springs from our fingers onto the recalcitrant helmets. Wordsworth wrote of lonely rooms, but he never wrote about third-floor people containing en-suite bathrooms.

The transferred epithet makes the world come alive. Prufrock's city mutters restlessly and Gray's fields tinkle drowsily. This is particularly true when the first noun is missing. You can say 'The nervous man smoked a cigarette'. You can say 'The man smoked a nervous cigarette'. But you can also say 'A nervous cigarette was smoked'. Dizzy heights and guilty secrets can stand on their own. The man has vanished altogether. All that's left are objects with human emotions.

Charles Dickens would have been the greatest master of the transferred epithet, except that he rarely used it. He went much, much further:

> Mr Jaggers never laughed; but he wore great bright creaking boots; and, in poising himself on these boots, with his large head bent down and his eyebrows joined together, awaiting an answer he sometimes caused the boots to creak, as if they laughed in a dry and suspicious way.

It's as though Dickens tried using the transferred epithet and then decided, 'It's not enough. I need more!' So he went and built a world in which all objects are alive. In Dickens' strange mind, mists were lazy, houses crazy, and snowflakes went into mourning and wore black. It's terrifying and it's beautiful, but the simple movement of the adjective has been left far behind. You can never tell, when Dickens talks about a threatening house or a miserable mist, whether anybody was meant to have these emotions in the first place. This was not the classic transferred epithet, it was the dark heart of Dickens' mind, and we should leave in a hurry.

The transferred epithet has very vague borders. Do happy days and lonely nights count? What about a knowing smile or sarcastic laugh? When Brutus stabbed Caesar and Shakespeare wrote:

This was the most unkindest cut of all

I can't decide whether that's a transferred epithet or just an accurate description of a cut. But it is certainly a case of pleonasm.

Chapter 31

—∞∞∞—

Pleonasm

Pleonasm is the use of unneeded words that are superfluous and unnecessary in a sentence that doesn't require them. It's repeating the same thing again twice, and it annoys and irritates people. Some cannot see a pleonasm without flying into a furious rage. But that is rather silly. There are three different varieties of pleonasm: the tiny, the lazy, and the lovely.

Let us start with the tiny. Psalm 121 begins thus:

I will lift up mine eyes unto the hills, from whence cometh my help.

There are people who would find that line inspiring. They would read it and run off to live better lives of purity and holiness up a hill somewhere. There are others who would find it infuriating. Twice. They would read it and as they did so the veins would stand out on their furious foreheads, the saliva would drip from their maddened mouths, and they would take a big red marker pen out of their pockets and delete two words.

First, there's the word 'up'. What other direction can you lift something? It's almost as bad as 'fall down' or 'enter into'. It is (some would say) an insult to the intelligence and an abuse of the English language. But it's not nearly as bad as 'from whence'. *Whence* means *from where*. So what does 'from whence' mean?

'From from where'? It's enough to make you shoot yourself, and then write an angry letter to the paper.

People who think like this lead terrible lives. They have never married, simply because they couldn't bear to hear the words:

> **Dearly beloved**, we are **gathered together** in the sight of God, and in the face of this congregation, to **join together** this man and this woman in Holy Matrimony …

They can't enjoy *Hamlet* because of the unnecessary 'that' in 'To be or not to be, that is the question'. And they can't even throw themselves in front of a train and put an end to their lives of misery and woe, because they're not sure about *railway tracks*.

The reason usually given for such anger is that the unnecessary word, the pleonasm, is wasting the reader's time. As though anybody's time were so valuable that reading the word 'up' might mess up their schedule. Those with the time to complain about time-wasting have too much time on their hands.

The second kind of pleonasm is quite different. It's the lazy adjective noun. This is a world of personal friends, added bonuses and free gifts. They are annoying for two contradictory reasons: first of all nobody talks like that, and secondly everybody talks like that.

I have never said the words 'free gift'. It would seem a sinister thing to say when gathered around the Christmas tree. 'Here's my free gift, and, as an added bonus, here's a festive Christmas card.' People would think I'd gone mad. Yet, if you wander into a shop or make the terrible mistake of turning on the television or radio, you will hear of havens that are safe, co-operation that is mutual, and prizes that are, it turns out, to be won.

Such phrases lumber about the language like zombies. They were created long ago by insanely evil marketing executives who were desperate to progress forward and sell their foreign imports to the general public. But, like Frankenstein's monster, they could not be stopped. They still lurk in shops and howl from televisions; even though their original inventor is past history.

And finally, there is the third and best kind of pleonasm: the lovely pleonasm of emphasis. A free gift may be put down to thoughtlessness, but 'free, gratis and for nothing' is quite deliberate. It is certainly pleonasm, but it is also effective. It is the pneumatic drill of repetition that gives emphasis and insistence to the notion that you don't have to pay a penny. A pedant may scream at the phrase 'I saw it with my own two eyes', but in conversation it means something. When Shakespeare wrote of 'Th'inaudible and noiseless foot of time', it wasn't that he hadn't thought it through. It was the same deliberate mind that had Hamlet complain:

> How weary, stale, flat and unprofitable
> Seem to me all the uses of this world.

We are all casual creatures and we say things that we don't really mean; so, when we really mean a thing, we say it twice. Or three times. Or sixteen times in a single speech, if you're complaining about a dead parrot that is:

1. Passed on
2. No more
3. Ceased to be
4. Expired

5. Gone to meet its maker
6. Stiff
7. Bereft of life
8. Rests in peace

And so on and so forth until we get to …

16. Ex

This is pleonasm, but it's pleonasm for an effect. The tragic truth of the parrot's mortality can be communicated only through repetition. And the only comfort can be found in the funeral service's 'sure and certain hope of the resurrection', where the pleonasm's power is set against the fragile 'hope'.

Pleonasm is absolutely natural and absolutely necessary. Kipling was undoubtedly being pleonastic when he wrote:

> Oh, East is East, and West is West, and never the twain
>   shall meet,
> Till Earth and Sky stand presently at God's great
>   Judgment Seat.

But you cannot take a red marker pen to that sentence without destroying it. Kipling needed to insist that East really, truly, actually was East; and that West really, truly, actually, factually was West. All Kipling was doing here was restating, rather memorably, the Law of Identity. The idea that a thing is itself dates back to the days of Socrates, Aristotle, togas and casual pederasty. It was formulated by Gottfried Leibniz as 'A is A'. This truth of logic is unchanging, a point demonstrated by the twentieth-century thinker Herman Hupfeld who asserted that:

A kiss is still a kiss,
A sigh is just a sigh;

But for pure pleonasm nobody has ever beaten Gertrude Stein, who took the trouble to point out in her poem 'Sacred Emily' that a 'Rose is a rose is a rose is a rose'.

This was, by far, Stein's most famous line. It's been adapted and parodied a million and one times, most memorably by Ernest Hemingway, who fell out with Miss Stein and wrote, 'A bitch is a bitch is a bitch is a bitch'. Stein reused the line herself, and added an 'A' to the beginning just in case anybody thought that she wasn't being pleonastic and was just describing a girl whose name was Rose. Stein's girlfriend, Alice Toklas, took to marketing dinner plates that had the phrase written all the way around the edge. The crockery version has no beginning and no end and is therefore a case of infinite pleonasm. That's only possible, of course, because the last word of the sentence is the same as the first word, which makes it an example of epanalepsis.

Chapter 32

—◦∞◦—

Epanalepsis

John Lennon complained that the song 'Yesterday' didn't go anywhere. You find out that the guy's unhappy, and that he longs for the past, but it never goes beyond that. There's no resolution. Lennon was quite right. After all, the song begins with the word 'yesterday' and ends 125 words later with the word 'yesterday'.

It's a circular song, which ends where it began. And it even does it at a smaller level. The first verse begins and ends with the same word – 'yesterday' – and so does the second – 'suddenly' – and so does the third – 'yesterday' again. But that's probably the song's strength. It's about a man who can't think of anything else but yesterday, and the words mirror that rather beautifully. It's also a double case of epanalepsis: beginning and ending with the same word.

Ending where you began has two effects that are, at first sight, contradictory. It gives the impression of going nowhere, and it gives the impression of moving inevitably on. So each New Year's Day you're back where you started: 1 January. And each New Year's Day an old year is gone for ever and a new one is upon you. Time moves ever onwards, and Time scampers around in circles. It's the same thing with epanalepsis.

'The king is dead; long live the king' sums up both sides of epanalepsis. On the one hand it announces that the old monarch is dead and gone, and that there is a new king on the throne. On the other hand, it curtly tells republicans that there will always be a monarch. Everything has changed, and everything has remained the same.[1]

Epanalepsis implies circularity and continuation. When Robert Burns wrote of 'Man's inhumanity to man' he didn't say that that inhumanity breeds inhumanity, but he implied it with the epanalepsis. It sounds so like 'A lie begets a lie' or 'Nothing will come of nothing' that we can't help feeling that there's an unending inhuman circle of dog eat dog eat dog eat dog. The phrase wouldn't have been nearly as memorable if Burns had written 'Man's inhumanity to others'.

'Man's inhumanity to man' is only one clause of one sentence. But epanalepsis can work at any scale you like. Paul McCartney finished his song by repeating a word; but Lewis Carroll finished his poem 'Jabberwocky' by repeating the whole of the first verse. It has the same effect, though. The Jabberwock may be slain, but it's still brillig, the toves are still slithy, and the mome raths continue their outgrabing. Everything has changed, but everything is still the same.

Of course, epanalepsis doesn't have to be used to imply circularity and continuation, it's just at its best when it does. Shakespeare wrote that 'men of few words are the best men', but it's not a particularly memorable line. Nor is 'Cassius from bondage will deliver Cassius'. Even his extended versions didn't catch on. Nobody remembers:

Blood hath bought blood and blows have answered blows;
Strength matched with strength, and power confronted power:

---

[1] Except, of course, when there's a Queen, at which point the epanalepsis is ruined.

But that's probably because nobody reads *King John*. There are times when Shakespeare seems to have given up on epanalepsis altogether. In *Julius Caesar* he has a battle of the speeches. Antony gives his 'Friends, Romans, countrymen' in answer to Brutus' much less famous 'Romans, countrymen and lovers' speech. Frankly, the term 'lovers' is a bit weird when addressing a large crowd of unwashed Romans. Shakespeare made Brutus' speech deliberately bad. And he filled it with epanalepsis.

> Romans, countrymen, and lovers! hear me for my cause, and be silent, that you may hear: believe me for mine honour, and have respect to mine honour, that you may believe:

It's as though Shakespeare was sick and tired of a rhetorical figure that had never really worked for him. But he didn't give up on it entirely. He hit the jackpot with epanalepsis once, out on a blasted heath, with an old man shouting at the weather.

If you think about it, writing a play involving wind and rain is a bold move in a world before fans and hosepipes. King Lear has to magic up his own scenery and storm. The weather was in the poetry, and Shakespeare seemed to like the challenge. He pulled out epanalepsis, not because of its circularity, but because of the pure emphasis on repetition. Lear's epanalepsis is one of command. It's the sort of sentence uttered by somebody who is used to being obeyed, and gets angry when he isn't.

> Blow, winds, and crack your cheeks! rage! blow!

Which is also an example of Shakespearean personification.

Chapter 33

⸺◦⦿◦⸺

Personification[1]

Personification is strange woman. She wanders about holding a mask and talking to herself. She's never there when you think she is, and when she does turn up, she tries to take over your life. But most importantly, she's very, very hard to define. Women, eh?

Duty calls, money talks, sleep beckons, and work phoned up to see if you could come in on Saturday. All of these are, technically, personifications. But they don't follow through. 'That was work on the phone' is an utterly natural phrase. But it would be followed by '*they* want me to come in on Saturday'. Not he or she. 'Work' there is something like a group noun, or a synecdoche (q.v.). It's not a human figure with eyes and lips and legs and bad breath.

Work personified could be a beautiful figure. He would be a large cruel man, I think, with a schedule in one hand and a whip in the other. He would wear a suit with money stuffed in the pockets. He would be invincible except when he did battle with the beautiful Lady Public Holiday who would arrive from the seaside on a white horse holding an ice cream and a broken alarm clock. They would fight in the stadium of …

---

[1] The Greek term, since you ask, is prosopopoeia. But for once we have a nice, normal English word that does the trick without lining up innumerable vowels.

But I'm getting carried away. Work is not personified in the phrase 'work phoned'. And money is not personified just before it talks. Duty calls but we never really hear its gruff voice. Necessity is the mother of invention, but did she have an epidural?

At the other end of the spectrum there's allegory. Allegory is proper personification, in fact it's personification that has moved in and taken over the whole story. In allegory the person isn't just suggested by a human verb, it's fleshed out and dressed up and given a house to live in. The best-known example in English is *The Pilgrim's Progress*, where a chap subtly named Christian meets a giant called Despair (and his wife, Diffidence) and gets bogged down in symbolic bogs and climbs a hill called Difficulty and so on and so forth until any sensible person is bored to tears.

Now, there's nothing wrong with allegory of this kind, but it has no place in this book. Here we are dealing only with the effects that can be achieved in a single sentence, or at most a paragraph. Allegory is for finer minds than mine, and deeper souls. Also, it tends to religion. Not just because the best examples are religious, but because personification is very close to deification. People worship money and nature, or rather Money and Nature, and turn them quickly into goddesses or gods. It's often hard to see whether they really mean it. In *King Lear* Edmund says:

Thou, nature, art my goddess; to thy law
My services are bound.

And you can't quite tell whether he means it. After all, the Ancient Romans worshipped Love (Venus) and War (Mars) and ironmongery (Vulcan), and it's not entirely clear to what extent they were personifications or gods or both and neither. It probably depended on the Ancient Roman.

So at one end, we have personification that barely exists, and at the other we have personification that's gone too far for us. Or, to put it another way, personification wears invisible shoes and a huge, flowery hat. Yet somewhere in between, somewhere around the nether regions, we have the personification that really works, and of which Shakespeare was the greatest master.

In *Othello* Iago warns Othello about jealousy.

O, beware, my lord, of jealousy;
It is the green-eyed monster which doth mock
The meat it feeds on;

Iago could just have called jealousy a monster. It would have done the job. There's no particular reason to mention the eye colour, but it's just enough to bring the monster to life. It's only a glimpse, a moment's revelation; but there it is, the real monster, suddenly glaring out at you. And then the peep-hole, which was opened for a moment, is slammed shut and we're back with Othello and Iago sitting in a room in Cyprus, discussing handkerchiefs.

Shakespeare had tried the trick before. Like many of his best lines he took a couple of stabs at it. A few years before, in *The Merchant of Venice*, he'd had 'shuddering fear, and green-eyed jealousy', but the problem with that line is that it's not *necessarily* a personification. It could just be that jealousy makes your eyes turn green. If I say that I'm in a 'wild-eyed panic' that just means that I'm wild-eyed.

Either way, Shakespeare had been honing this technique since his earliest plays. Eyes and faces, glimpsed for a moment, and then gone. Just a brush from Personification's elbow as she dashes by. Contrast and compare:

'Bold-faced Victory' (*Henry VI Part 1*)
'Close-tongued Treason' (*The Rape of Lucrece*)
'Open-eyed Conspiracy' (*The Tempest*)
'Fire-eyed Fury' (*Romeo and Juliet*)
'The silver hand of Peace' (*Henry IV Part 2*)
'Pale-faced Fear' (*Henry VI Part 1*)
'The iron tongue of Midnight'
  (*A Midsummer Night's Dream*)
'Smooth-faced peace' (*Richard III*)
'That smooth-faced gentleman, tickling Commodity'
  (*King John*)

And on and on and on. And people tell you that Shakespeare was inspired. He practised. Each one has a person, a visible person, leap into existence, be glimpsed, and vanish. Usually he used a single body-part to imply the whole, but sometimes he gave his abstraction a house. In *Henry VI Part 2* we glimpse, for one line, 'Lean-faced Envy in her loathsome cave'. And then we leave her there, not even knowing why she was a woman.

But two persons stalk through all Shakespeare's plays: Time and Death. Each is seen only in glimpses. Time's foot is inaudible, his hand is cruel, and he carries a sickle. Death is a fuller figure. He's a shrunken carcass, a carrion, he wears rags but his ribs are bare. He carries a pale flag and wears a black veil over his loathsome visage. And he eats people. Shakespeare's Death doesn't lead people away to an afterlife, he munches them in his steel jaws, an eternal feast that takes place in the eternal cell in his secret house in a melancholy vale. Death also has sex. Not often, but he does. Cleopatra is understandable. But Juliet too:

> O son! the night before thy wedding-day
> Hath Death lain with thy wife. There she lies,
> Flower as she was, deflowered by him.
> Death is my son-in-law, Death is my heir;
> My daughter he hath wedded: I will die,
> And leave him all; life, living, all is Death's.

And then he eats her.

What this tells us about Shakespeare's psyche, I don't know and don't want to know. The important thing is that you only get this complete picture of hungry, randy, ragged death if you read the whole of Shakespeare's works and put it together. Because Shakespeare does it all in glimpses. One detail and then Death is hidden away again. It's beautiful and it's remarkably effective. This isn't the half-personification of 'duty calls', but it's not the full-blown allegory either. It's one detail and no more.

Unfortunately this technique pretty much died with Shakespeare. There are a few examples since, and each one has been beautiful. Andrew Marvell gave Time a mode of transport:

> But at my back I always hear
> Time's wingèd chariot hurrying near

Imagine if it had been:

> Relentless Time still hurrying near

The whole beauty of the line would have been lost. But as long as you have that one wingèd chariot, you have an image. 'The awakening Morn' wouldn't be anything much. So Milton wrote:

> For we were nursed upon the self-same hill,
> Fed the same flock, by fountain, shade, and rill.
> Together both, ere the high Lawns appeared
> Under the opening eye-lids of the morn

Mind you, Milton stole that from the Book of Job, which has 'the eyelids of the morning', but he stole it well.

And then Personification became less popular. She stayed home more and more, and grew ill. Keats tried to take her on a few dates, but she grew pale, and spectre-thin, and died. Duty still calls, money still talks, and work still phones up; but Personification isn't what she used to be. Poor girl.

She's not quite dead, though. That would be an overstatement.

Chapter 34

⟋∞⟍

Hyperbole

Hyperbole (pronounced hi-PER-boh-lee) is the technical term for exaggeration, and even though we have literally thousands of English words that mean the same thing, hyperbole is one of the few technical Greek rhetorical terms that absolutely everybody knows.

That may be because we exaggerate constantly. The human being is the great embroiderer. It's not enough for us to say that we waited for ten minutes; we have to wait 'for ages'. If I've told you twice, I've told you a thousand times. If you're rich, you have a ton of money. It's enough to make you break down in a flood of tears.

However, we do not use hyperbole enough. We lack ambition. The state of Kansas is actually flatter than a pancake.[1] It's quite possible to have a ton of money. All you need is £2,853.93 in coppers. If you really want to make a hyperbole work, you must make sure that it is beyond anything that is even vaguely possible. What is the point in a mere ton of money? Damon Runyon (who called money 'potatoes' as that was the New York slang of the time) went much further:

> [A]nybody who ever reads the newspapers will tell you that Miss Abigail Ardsley has so many potatoes that it is really

---

[1] See Fonstad, Pugatch, Vogt, 2003, *The Annals of Improbable Research*, Vol. 9.

painful to think of, especially to people who have no potatoes whatever. In fact, Miss Abigail Ardsley has practically all the potatoes in the world, except maybe a few left over for general circulation.

That's a lot of potatoes, and that's a proper hyperbole. Given that people recognise an exaggeration when they hear one, you might as well go for it. At the same time that Runyon was describing money on the East Coast, Dashiell Hammett was describing private detectives on the West.

> He was a swarthy little Canadian who stood nearly five feet in his high-heeled shoes, weighed a hundred pounds minus, talked like a Scotchman's telegram, and could have shadowed a drop of salt water from Golden Gate to Hongkong without ever losing sight of it.

Indeed, the Americans seem to be the modern masters of the impossible hyperbole. Next to their mountainous over-statements, an Englishman's languid and effete attempts are subatomically small.

Yet there was a time when the English could do that sort of hyperbole too. Long, long ago, at a time when the Big Bang was still a recent and painful memory, lived a man called Sydney Smith (1771–1845). One day, Reverend Smith was informed that a chap who lived down the road had got engaged to a lady who was not exactly skinny. His response was not exactly gentlemanly, but it was properly hyperbolic.

Marry her! Impossible! You mean a part of her; he could not marry her all himself. It would be a case not of bigamy, but trigamy; the neighbourhood or the magistrates should interfere. There is enough of her to furnish wives for a whole parish. One man marry her! – it is monstrous. You might people a colony with her; or give an assembly with her; or perhaps take your morning walk round her, always provided there were frequent resting places, and you were in rude health. I once was rash enough to try walking round her before breakfast, but only got half-way, and gave it up exhausted. Or you might read the Riot Act and disperse her; in short, you might do anything with her but marry her.

Next to these heroic efforts, most of Shakespeare's exaggerations seem like understatements. The best he could do for 'You're very fat' was his description of Falstaff as 'this horseback-breaker, this huge hill of flesh'. It's hardly enough. He had his moments, of course; Shakespeare usually did.

Will all great Neptune's ocean wash this blood
Clean from my hand? No, this my hand will rather
The multitudinous seas in incarnadine,
Making the green one red.

But that is mainly memorable for the strange verb *incarnadine*. For top-grade hyperbole we need to go back and consult the Son of God.

And why do you look at the speck in your brother's eye, but do not consider the plank in your own eye? Or how can you

say to your brother, 'Let me remove the speck from your eye';
and look, a plank is in your own eye? Hypocrite! First remove
the plank from your own eye, and then you will see clearly to
remove the speck from your brother's eye.

All things are, of course, possible with Jesus, but having a large
plank of wood in your eye and not noticing is an extreme
example. It's almost as silly as trying to get a whole camel
through the eye of a needle, which is an impossibility, or, to put
it technically, an adynaton.

Chapter 35

∞

Adynaton

**And again I say unto you, It is easier for a camel
to go through the eye of a needle, than for a rich
man to enter into the kingdom of God.**
Matthew 19, verse 24

This verse has always rather worried rich men,[1] who tend to ask themselves how much a really damned big needle would cost. There's a pretty theory that there was once a Needle Gate in the walls of Jerusalem that camels could get through, provided they went down on their knees. Unfortunately for the rich, it's utterly untrue; but it's a nice idea.

Even the disciples, who were a pretty low-income lot, 'were exceedingly amazed, saying, Who then can be saved?' To which Jesus comfortingly replied that 'with God all things are possible'. Jesus' importance for rhetoric is therefore that he didn't believe in adynata.

An adynaton (pronounced ad-in-ART-on) is impossible. Before an adynaton will work, pigs will fly, Hell will freeze over and the Devil will go skiing. You might as well try to get blood out of a stone. It's therefore a very easy, if very periphrastic, way of saying no.

---

[1] Rich women, it seems, are in the clear.

John Donne could have written that honesty gets you nowhere. Instead, he wrote:

> Go and catch a falling star,
> Get with child a mandrake root,
> Tell me where all past years are,
> Or who cleft the devil's foot,
> Teach me to hear mermaids singing,
> Or to keep off envy's stinging,
>   And find
>   What wind
> Serves to advance an honest mind.

Similarly the sentence 'I'm not going to go out with that girl again; she's from Scarborough' is a trifle tedious. But if you instead agree to take her back if she can perform three impossible tasks, you can have some fun. You can demand that she make you a cambric shirt without using needle and thread, that she finds you an acre of land between the sea and the shore, and that she reaps it with a leather sickle. Chuck in some parsley, sage, rosemary and thyme and bingo. You've got yourself a folk song, although not a Scarborian girlfriend.

Any negative can be transformed into an adynaton. There tend to be two forms: 'you might as well try to …' and 'not until …'. However, they're pretty interchangeable. A supporter of Ulysses S. Grant predicted the result of the 1869 Presidential election thus:

> Build a worm-fence round a winter supply of summer weather;
> catch a thunder-bolt in a bladder; break a hurricane to harness;

hang out the ocean on a grape-vine to dry; but never, sir, never for a moment delude yourself with the idea that you can beat Grant.

But he could just as well have phrased it: 'When you've managed to build a worm-fence [etc. etc. etc.] then you'll beat Grant.' Conversely you could take W.H. Auden's exclamation of undying love:

> 'I'll love you, dear, I'll love you
> Till China and Africa meet,
> And the river jumps over the mountain
> And the salmon sing in the street,
>
> 'I'll love you till the ocean
> Is folded and hung up to dry
> And the seven stars go squawking
> Like geese about the sky.'[2,3]

And change it to 'I'm about as likely to stop loving you as …'.

The important thing is that, in terms of content, Auden's lines only say 'I'll always love you'. The adynata are purely adornments. They're verbal fun. They're Auden sitting around dreaming up impossibilities and making them rhyme.

Adynaton is just Greek for 'impossible', but that doesn't mean that anything impossible is an adynaton, because in

---

[2] 'As I Walked Out One Evening'. Copyright © 1940. By W.H. Auden, renewed. Reprinted by permission of Curtis Brown, Ltd.

[3] While we're at it, you may also want to notice the diacope, polysyndeton, catachresis, alliteration and anaphora (q.v.).

rhetoric adynaton is just a long way round of saying 'this is the case'. Almost any sentence can have an adynaton added in. 'My name is Mark Forsyth' can become 'If my name isn't Mark Forsyth, may the crayfish whistle on the mountainside' (which is, apparently, the Russian equivalent of pigs might fly).

So when Auden reused the image of the sea drying up in 'Funeral Blues':[4,5]

> Pour away the ocean and sweep up the wood
> For nothing now can ever come to any good.

… it's not an adynaton, he was just being sad. The same goes for Chesterton's 'When fishes flew and forests walked', or for the great Mormon Sex In Chains case of 1977, where a former Miss Wyoming abducted and ravaged a Mormon missionary, later stating: 'I loved Kirk so much I would have skied down Mount Everest in the nude with a carnation up my nose.' That's not a proper rhetorical adynaton, it's just love.

Sometimes, the lines get a bit blurry. The famous graffito, 'A woman needs a man like a fish needs a bicycle', is kind of an adynaton, and kind of not. And sometimes something can be a rhetorical adynaton without really being impossible. Hamlet's poem of true love to Ophelia was meant to describe a series of impossibilities:

---

[4] Copyright © 1940. By W.H. Auden, renewed. Reprinted by permission of Curtis Brown, Ltd.

[5] Burns had the same line: 'Till a' the seas gang dry, my dear, / And the rocks melt wi' the sun.' But the adynaton is rather overdone – impossibility is one thing, but warm sunshine in Scotland is ridiculous.

Doubt thou the stars are fire;
Doubt that the sun doth move;
Doubt truth to be a liar;
But never doubt I love.

But the Danish Prince was unfortunate in all things. First Copernicus put paid to the moving sun, and then Arthur Eddington in 1920 pointed out that stars are not fire, but instead produce their light through the fusion of hydrogen to helium. If Ophelia had had even a passing knowledge of modern astrophysics she would have realised that their relationship was doomed.

In the prologue to the medieval religious dream poem *Piers Plowman*, the poet says that you 'Might as well measure the mist on Malvern Hills'[6] as get a lawyer to talk without first paying him a fee. Unfortunately there is now a weather station on Malvern Hills, and the humidity is measured and reported.[7]

It's sad to see Time's toothless mouth laughing the poets to scorn. The stars are all explained and the mist is all measured, and there is no magic left in this dreary world. But the legal profession still charge exorbitant fees. That at least is a truth we can cling to. After all, Shakespeare's first famous line, as we have seen, was 'The first thing we do, let's kill all the lawyers'.

Which is an example of prolepsis.

---

[6] 'Thou mightest beter meten the myst on Malverne hulles / Then geten a mom of heore mouth til moneye be schewed.'

[7] www.malvernwx.co.uk/Graphs/2013/2013_humidity.gif

Chapter 36

⸺ ✺ ⸺

Prolepsis

They're simple things, pronouns. Your English teacher probably explained them to you like this. You use a **noun** and afterwards, when you want to refer to **it**, you can use a pronoun, like 'it'. The reader knows what the **pronoun** refers to because **it** appeared earlier in the sentence. Or **it** appeared earlier in the paragraph.

About pronouns **they** were sometimes wrong, **the old masters**; because you can use a pronoun before saying what it refers to. It's an odd little technique, and it's called prolepsis.[1]

It's perfectly natural, prolepsis. We use it all the time in conversation, but we rarely write it down. Somehow the rules that our teachers taught us reach out their chalky hands and stop the pen. It takes a very good poet to unlearn the rules. When we do, the effect is remarkable. After all:

They fuck you up, your mum and dad.
They may not mean to, but they do.

---

[1] Most rhetorical terms are awkward (see Epilogue), but prolepsis is one of the worst as it has five more rhetorical or grammatical meanings that are pretty much unrelated, as *prolepsis* is merely the Greek for 'anticipation'. So it can also mean *anticipating your opponent's argument*: 'He'll probably tell you X, but I can prove that X is wrong.' It can also mean *referring to something in its future state*: 'You're a dead man walking.' It can be a form of irony where a character in a play says something that later turns out to be untrue. It can be a grammatical construction in which a verb agrees with a whole but not the parts. It can mean a rhetorical device in which the subject is outlined in brief before being dealt with in detail: 'This paper will show that …' It also has a couple of medical and botanical meanings.

is not an amazing observation, especially for an observer of Philip Larkin's talents. (I, for one, would replace the F with a B.) But even if you take the Freudian view and agree with the content, many would baulk at the coarse simplification of the message. Nonetheless, it's one of the most famous first lines in twentieth-century poetry. To work out why, you just need to see what it would look like without the prolepsis:

Your mum and dad, they fuck you up

Or, if you insist on keeping the rhyme:

You're fucked up by your mum and dad

But no. They've lost it, those alternatives, they've lost it good and proper. The mysterious prolepsis always gives you a good line, especially a first one. Philip Larkin (1971) had probably learnt that lesson from the first line of Stevie Smith's 'Not Waving But Drowning' (1957), which uses exactly the same technique for its first line:

Nobody heard him, the dead man,
But still he lay moaning;

And Stevie Smith had probably learnt it from the first line of W.H. Auden's 'Musée Des Beaux Arts'[2] (1938), which uses exactly the same technique:

---

[2] Copyright © 1940. By W.H. Auden, renewed. Reprinted by permission of Curtis Brown, Ltd.

About suffering they were never wrong,
The old Masters: how well they understood …

And W.H. Auden had probably learnt it from the first line of
Ernest Dowson's 'Vitae Summa Brevis' (1896), which uses
exactly the same technique again:

They are not long, the weeping and the laughter,
Love and desire and hate;
I think they have no portion in us after
We pass the gate.

And then repeats it for the even more famous second verse:

They are not long, the days of wine and roses,
Out of a misty dream
Our path emerges for a while, then closes
Within a dream.

Prolepsis has two great advantages. First, it has mystery, but not
too much. When a poem opens with a pronoun, a little bit of
your mind thinks to itself: 'What? What the hell's going on? Who?
Who are *they*?' For a moment it weeps and wonders, but only for
a moment, because a few words later, before the full stop is even
upon us, you find out that they are the old masters, or your mum
and dad, or the days of wine and roses. The mystery is opened,
your attention is grabbed, and then the mystery is solved.

This sort of thing can go horribly wrong if you get too ambitious with your mystery pronouns. There's a certain kind of
thriller novel that always opens:

There were three of them. He'd known that all along. But why had she sent them? He thought of telling them that he didn't have it any more, any of it. But if they knew those were gone, they might tell her that he didn't have them. Then he'd really be for it.

Such openings drive any sane reader insane, and only play into the hands of book-burners. But the principle is sound, and used much more subtly and successfully by the greatest poets in the English language.

The second reason that prolepsis is so effective is that it is thoughtful and natural. We have all, after thinking about something for a while, lost in meditation, suddenly said something like 'That's it!' or 'They're all in it together!' or 'She couldn't possibly have known that, at the time of the murder, the clocks would all have been turned back an hour.' And then, noticing that there are others in the room who won't have understood what we're talking about, we add an explanatory noun: 'Beer' or 'the CIA and the cartels' or 'Lady Chlamydia Glossop'. So when Auden starts his poem with 'About suffering they were never wrong', it's as though he's actually been sitting in the Musée Des Beaux Arts, staring at a painting and lost in thought. And when he says 'The old Masters', it's as though he's suddenly realised he's been talking aloud, and now wishes to explain himself.

Similarly, you can imagine somebody standing at dawn on Westminster Bridge, looking at London. After a while, he says, to nobody in particular, 'Earth has not anything to show more fair'. He doesn't mention what the *anything* is, because he's talking to himself, still caught up in the fairness of it all. Then he notices you, and, by way of justification, adds:

Dull would he be of soul who could pass by
A sight so touching in its majesty:
This City now doth, like a garment, wear
The beauty of the morning; silent, bare,
Ships, towers, domes, theatres and temples lie
Open unto the fields, and to the sky

To which a cruel passer-by would say, 'If it's wearing the morning like a garment, how come it's bare? Eh?' But a more understanding soul would say: 'Ships, towers, domes, theatres, and temples. Well done, Mr Wordsworth. That's a lovely congeries.'

Chapter 37

—— ∞∞∞ ——

Congeries

The best thing about congeries is that it's a singular noun. Otherwise I'd use the word 'list'. List means exactly the same thing, but it has none of the exoticism of congeries, no spice, no adventure, no derring-do, no whiff of the palm tree and the jungle, no pizzazz, no fairy-dust, no magic. Also everybody knows how to pronounce 'list', but no two dictionaries can agree on congeries, which makes it much more fun. The plural, incidentally is congeries.

Congeries is Latin for a heap, and in rhetoric it applies to any piling up of adjectives or nouns in a list. So when St Paul said:

Now the works of the flesh are manifest, which are these; Adultery, fornication, uncleanness, lasciviousness, Idolatry, witchcraft, hatred, variance, emulations, wrath, strife, seditions, heresies, Envyings, murders, drunkenness, revellings, and such like [...] But the fruit of the Spirit is love, joy, peace, longsuffering, gentleness, goodness, faith, Meekness, temperance ...

He was making a congeries. He was also doing something completely unnatural, because humans don't naturally make lists. Or, to be more precise, we don't talk in lists. If I were to ask what your 50 favourite films were, you would probably settle down with a pencil and paper and spend an hour or so puzzling over it. If I didn't let you have any stationery, you'd start to talk, but you'd talk very, very slowly. You'd roll your eyes around and look at the ceiling for inspiration. So would I. So would anybody.

If you took one deep breath and reeled off the full list in one, syllable-perfect, and in ascending order, I would think you either a superhuman, or the sort of person who has worked it all out with pencil and paper some lonely Sunday and then memorised it in the hope, in the desperate hope, that you would someday be asked Just That Question. Either way, I would think you peculiar. Nobody but a God or a fool talks in lists.

Which is why they are so effective. They startle and bewilder. If a normal person were asked to describe a Christmas tree they would murmur something about presents and tinsel. Here is how Dickens did it:

The tree was planted in the middle of a great round table, and towered high above their heads. It was brilliantly lighted by a multitude of little tapers; and everywhere sparkled and glittered with bright objects. There were rosy-cheeked dolls, hiding behind the green leaves; and there were real watches (with movable hands, at least, and an endless capacity of being wound up) dangling from innumerable twigs; there were French-polished tables, chairs, bedsteads, wardrobes, eight-day clocks, and various other articles of domestic furniture (wonderfully made, in tin, at Wolverhampton), perched among the boughs, as if in preparation for some fairy housekeeping; there were jolly, broad-faced little men, much more agreeable in appearance than many real men – and no wonder, for their heads took off, and showed them to be full of sugar-plums; there were fiddles and drums; there were tambourines, books, work-boxes, paint-boxes, sweetmeat-boxes, peep-show boxes,[1] and all kinds of boxes; there were trinkets for the elder girls, far brighter than any grown-up gold and jewels; there were baskets and pincushions in all devices; there were guns, swords, and banners; there were witches standing in enchanted rings of pasteboard, to tell fortunes; there were teetotums, humming-tops, needle-cases, pen-wipers, smelling-bottles, conversation-cards, bouquet-holders; real fruit, made artificially dazzling with gold leaf; imitation apples, pears, and walnuts, crammed with surprises; in short, as a pretty child, before me, delightedly whispered to another pretty child, her bosom friend, 'There was everything, and more.'

That's a list, a list nobody could say or speak unless they had spent six months memorising it. But what an image! Noun after noun after noun. You cannot help but see the Christmas tree in all its detailed glory. It is a heap of pretty images. And that's how Dickens wanted to get his image across. The reader is simply bludgeoned into submission.

Congeries work precisely because readers and listeners aren't used to them. We can deal with gold-tongued flattery and snarled threats, but a list? It hits below the belt. And a list doesn't need to be as long as Dickens' Christmas tree.

---

[1] A 'peep-show box' in that more innocent age was a box with a magnifying glass in the side through which you could see little painted wonders. In the twentieth century some bright and drooling spark had the idea of putting dirty pictures inside, and eventually somebody decided to shove a whole girl in there. This is called Progress.

Shakespeare got the same sort of effect with:

> The cloud-capp'd towers, the gorgeous palaces,
> The solemn temples, the great globe itself

Shakespeare loved lists, especially when he was insulting people.

> … you starveling, you elf-skin, you dried neat's tongue, you bull's pizzle, you stock-fish! O for breath to utter what is like thee! You tailor's-yard, you sheath, you bowcase; you vile standing-tuck …

The technical name for a heap of insults is bdelygmia, and the best thing about a good bdelygmia (aside from the pronunciation: no letter is silent) is that you don't even need to know what any of the words mean. I have no idea what a tailor's-yard is, or why it might be an insult. Yet it works, as part of a list. Take this beauty from Gabriel Harvey in the late sixteenth century:

> Fie on impure Ganymedes, Hermaphrodites, Neronists, Messalinists, Dodecomechanists, Capricians, Inventors of new, or Revivers of old lecheries, and the whole brood of venereous libertines.

You would need a damned fine classical education to even have a hint of what you were being accused of. But as a bdelygmia, it's beautiful.

Of course, a congeries doesn't have to be made of nouns; adjectives will pummel just as well. They don't paint a picture in the way that nouns do, but they beat their way in. Shakespeare described sex and wanting to have sex thus:

> The expense of spirit[2] in a waste of shame
> Is lust in action: and till action, lust
> Is perjured, murderous, bloody, full of blame,
> Savage, extreme, rude, cruel, not to trust;

Which shows that the poor chap was probably as bad with women as he was good with words. A good list is the love of every good writer. Joyce rejoiced in them, Beckett revelled, Wilde went wild, and Homer counted ships. There is something liberating about simply putting together words with no need to bother with structuring them. Even when a congeries is simply found lying around it has a certain magic to it. Take this list from 1953 of words approved by the East German government for describing the British:

> Paralytic sycophants, effete betrayers of humanity, carrion-eating servile imitators, arch-cowards and collaborators, gang of woman-murderers, degenerate rabble, parasitic traditionalists, playboy soldiers, conceited dandies.

Splendid sentence. But no verb.

---

[2] Semen.

Chapter 38

Scesis Onomaton

Some people believe that a sentence has to have a main verb. Nonsense! It's quite possible to hold a long conversation without a verb in sight. 'Drink?' 'Thanks.' 'Your round.' 'Really?' 'Yes.' 'Damn.'

And it's quite possible to write without main verbs. You can't do it for ever, but you can have a go. No verbs. Only fragments. A noun here; a participle there. The first sentence of *Bleak House*.

London.

That's a good first sentence. That's a writer who knew what he wanted to say. He wanted to say London, and everything it stood for. Start there and then we can narrow down. The next sentence has no main verb either:

Michaelmas term lately over, and the Lord Chancellor sitting in Lincoln's Inn Hall.

Just to be clear, 'sitting' is a participle acting as an adjective to 'Lord Chancellor'. Then:

Implacable November weather.

And so it goes on. Ten more full stops. 343 more words until you finally get to a sentence with a main verb in it. Nothing actually does anything. It hangs there like fog. 'Fog everywhere.' The scene is set perfectly, because that's what scesis onomaton (SKEE-sis o-NO-mat-on) does best. Setting scenes. The simple noun that tells you all you need to know.

Space: the final frontier.

It wouldn't be nearly as good if it ran:

This is Space, which is the final frontier.

Who needs an 'is' when you have all those nouns? Eternity. A sentence without a tense. 'This is Space', 'this was Space', or 'this will be Space' would limit it in time. If you dispense with main verbs then it could be past, present or future. Dickens' London is, was and will be London. It doesn't matter what those in London now do with the city, because Dickens claimed it in one timeless word. His is a London where dinosaurs ruled the earth; he's quite explicit about it:

As much mud in the streets as if the waters had but newly retired from the face of the earth, and it would not be wonderful to meet a Megalosaurus, forty feet long or so, waddling like an elephantine lizard up Holborn Hill.

London: the eternal city. As timeless as *Star Trek*'s void. And when Dickens finally does get to a main verb (because you can't keep scesis onomaton up for ever), he deliberately throws his readers:

Most of the shops **lighted** two hours before their time – as the gas **seems** to know, for it **has** a haggard and unwilling look.

Past and present in one sentence. Dickens didn't want to be tied down to a time just yet. Scesis onomaton can therefore set an eternal scene, but it can also state an eternal principle, one that's not pinned down within History's muddy field. When Winston Churchill wrote his history of the Second World War he had a lot to say about the events of 1939–45, events that he had in large part brought about. But the book begins with a simple, verbless heading: 'The Moral of the Work'. And underneath that is written:

In War: Resolution.
In Defeat: Defiance.
In Victory: Magnanimity.
In Peace: Good Will.

He could have made it a boast: 'In war, I had resolution'; or a patriotic victory: 'We had resolution'. He could have made it an order along the lines of the Ten Commandments: 'In War thou shalt have resolution.' Or he could have made it a proclamation of the future: 'In War we shall always have resolution.' But any of those alternatives would have limited him, and limited his words. This was not the history. That would follow in Chapter 1. This was, is and will be The Moral of the Work and a moral has no time. No birth. No death.

Churchill's eternal truths were rather noble. But scesis onomaton works for even the pettiest rule. 'Finders keepers' does not deign to tell us whether they were, are, will be or should be. It's a rule, a verbless rule (and was actually an underlying principle of parts of the British Empire). The same goes for 'Each to his own', 'Like father, like son' and 'Third time lucky'.

This timeless aspect of scesis onomaton has been rather brought down by its use in politics. Few figures can last long in that world without being scalded by all the hot air. There have been enough protest placards calling for 'War!' or 'No War!', for 'Justice!' or, in minority cases, 'Injustice!', that the bare noun has started to look rather bare. Yet in other fields, the scesis onomaton still bears fruit. Tennyson used it for 'Crossing the Bar':

> Sunset and evening star,
>> And one clear call for me!

The verblessness is perfect for a poem about going 'from out our bourn of Time and Place'. But he uses it even more effectively as a closing. In *In Memoriam*, part 50, he runs through a whole poem of fully verbed-up sentences. So you aren't expecting the end. But as usual with Tennyson, mortality and eternity are the themes. Tennyson was a great poet, but I can't imagine that he was that much fun to spend a month with. All beard and misery. The last verse begins with a main verb and looks thoroughly traditional and grammatical:

> Be near me when I fade away,
>> To point the term of human strife,
>> And on the low dark verge of life
> The twilight of eternal day.

And time and verbs have vanished. Nothing to cling to. That is the great feat of scesis. Of course, it has other effects.

'Me Tarzan. You Jane' manages to avoid eternal truth. It also never popped up in any of the films, even as a clapper-board.

It's very hard to say what the most popular play of Renaissance London was. The longest single run of any play was Thomas Middleton's *A Game At Chess*, which ran for nine whole nights, at which point it was banned for being too politically interesting for contemporary audiences (and hence too tedious for anyone today). However, *A Game at Chess* wasn't famous for its memorable lines. That honour went to *The Spanish Tragedy* by Thomas Kyd.

The Spanish Tragedy stood in relation to Renaissance drama in the way that *Casablanca* stands in relation to cinema. It wasn't quite the first, but it was pretty much the first anyone cared about. It may not have been the best, but it was the classic. *Casablanca* was big and melodramatic in a way that you could get away with in the 1940s and that everyone still secretly loves, even if we feel we're too clever for it today. *The Spanish Tragedy* was big and melodramatic in a way you could get away with in the late 1580s, and that everyone still loved in 1610, even if they felt that they were too clever for it by then. People would get drunk and then recite the lines in a tearful manner. This happened enough that there were scenes in other plays taking the mickey out of how people re-enacted the scenes of *The Spanish Tragedy*.

Thomas Kyd was a hell of a writer. There is only one contemporary account of seeing *Hamlet* in the theatre. Not Shakespeare's version. Nobody thought that worth writing about. No. Thomas Kyd's original.[1] Not the Shakespeare remake.

---

[1] Most scholars seem to agree that the first *Hamlet* was probably written by Kyd, but there's no solid evidence. The only line that survives is 'Hamlet! Revenge!'

And *The Spanish Tragedy* was Kyd's best play and the best lines in *The Spanish Tragedy* were the main-verbless …

> O eyes! No eyes, but fountains fraught with tears!
> O life! No life, but lively form of death!
> O world! No world, but mass of public wrongs,
> Confused and filled with murder and misdeeds!
> O Heavens!

Which is a good example of isocolon, alliteration, metaphor, and anaphora.

———∞∞∞———

Chapter 39

Anaphora

Anaphora (an-AFF-or-a) is starting each sentence with the same words. It's the king of rhetorical figures. I hate to confess it, but it's true. Hendiadys has her eccentric charm, polyptoton slaves away in the background, catachresis wanders around smashing things up, but anaphora has all the power.

It's so preposterously easy to do. It's so preposterously easy to pick some words. It's so preposterously easy to repeat them. Everyone can do it. Everyone can start a sentence the same way. It takes no skill. It takes …

I could go on like this all day, and be thinking about something else. But anaphora is dangerous. It's almost too powerful. Or to put it more precisely, it's like a gun: very useful, but you need to point it the right way before pulling the trigger. With anaphora people always remember the opening words, but they usually forget the rest.

Do you remember Winston Churchill's description of the invasion of Britain? Do you remember how he spoke of the Germans defeating our navy, landing on the south coast, taking London and reducing British resistance to a few guerrilla fighters in Wales or the Lake District or somewhere like that? Do you remember that? No?

That's odd, because you do. You just never listened to the speech. You listened to the anaphora. Churchill used to write his speeches out on separate lines. So his description of the

German conquest of Britain, delivered to Parliament in 1940 when Britain stood alone, ally-less and facing almost certain defeat, would have looked, in his notes, like this:

> We shall not flag or fail.
> We shall go on to the end.
> We shall fight in France,
> We shall fight on the seas and oceans [North and Atlantic],
> We shall fight with growing confidence and growing strength
>   in the air,
> We shall defend our island, whatever the cost may be,
> We shall fight on the beaches [of Britain],
> We shall fight on the landing grounds [of Britain],
> We shall fight in the fields [of Kent] and in the streets
>   [of London],
> We shall fight in the hills [Somewhere up North].
> We shall never surrender.[1]

It's pretty clear what he's describing. He's describing defeat, defeat with honour.

But Churchill also knew exactly what he was doing with anaphora. People never hear the rest, they hear the words 'We shall fight' and that's good enough for them. They hear, and because they've heard it several times, they believe. Churchill needed to get across two messages: we shall fight, and we shall probably lose. The anaphora allowed him to push one, while slipping the other in unnoticed.

---

[1] This is part of a speech Churchill delivered to Parliament on 4 June 1940.

He phrased exactly the same thing privately to his Cabinet. But he told them: 'If at last the long story [of Britain] is to end, it were better it should end, not through surrender, but only when we are rolling senseless on the ground.'[2]

Do you remember Martin Luther King and his dream? Do you remember what the dream was? All the details? I mean, I'm sure you remember the speech in general. But what three states are named? No? Nobody remembers. They remember the dream and not the details.

Of course, anaphora doesn't have to use a whole phrase. You can get by with only a word. The effect is slightly less powerful, but beautifully hypnotic. There was an eighteenth-century poet called Christopher Smart. Smart did all of the things that you might expect of an eighteenth-century poet: getting into debt, writing scurrilous poems, writing religious poems, signing silly contracts with booksellers. In the end it all got too much for him and he was confined to a madhouse with nothing to keep him company except a cat called Jeoffrey.

So Smart wrote a poem. It's a very odd poem by any measure. For starters, it's in Free Verse, which wasn't really meant to exist back then. For seconds, it's utterly insane in a terribly religious way (lines like 'Let Samuel, the Minister from a child, without ceasing praise with the Porcupine, which is the creature of defence and stands upon his arms continually' should give you some idea). But the oddest thing is that all the lines on each page begin with the same word. On some pages this word is 'Let', and on other pages this word is 'For'.

---

[2] This line was noted down by Hugh Dalton, Minister of Economic Warfare, who also remembered it as: 'If this long island story of ours is to end at last, let it end only when each of us lies choking in his own blood upon the ground.'

So, in a sense, it's not free verse. Anaphora is the verse form. It is pure anaphoric poetry. And the most beautiful passage is the one about his cat, Jeoffrey.

> For he purrs in thankfulness, when God tells him he's a
>   good Cat.
> For he is an instrument for the children to learn
>   benevolence upon.
> For every house is incomplete without him and a blessing is
>   lacking in the spirit.
> For the Lord commanded Moses concerning the cats at
>   the departure of the Children of Israel from Egypt.
> For every family had one cat at least in the bag.
> For the English Cats are the best in Europe.
> For he is the cleanest in the use of his fore-paws of any
>   quadruped.
> For the dexterity of his defence is an instance of the love
>   of God to him exceedingly.
> For he is the quickest to his mark of any creature.
> For he is tenacious of his point.
> For he is a mixture of gravity and waggery.
> For he knows that God is his Saviour.

For without all those *for*s, this wouldn't be much of a read. For without all those *for*s, it would be the ravings of a madman. For with all those *for*s, it is, at least, the ravings of a mad poet.

Anaphora gets everywhere. It's been running through this book. Every chapter, every figure, every writer. Do you remember Dickens' fog?

Fog everywhere. Fog up the river, where it flows among green aits and meadows; fog down the river [...] Fog on the Essex marshes, fog on the Kentish heights. Fog creeping into the cabooses of collier-brigs; fog lying out on the yards and hovering in the rigging of great ships; fog drooping on the gunwales of barges and small boats. Fog in the eyes and throats of ancient Greenwich pensioners, wheezing by the firesides of their wards; fog in the stem and bowl of the afternoon pipe of the wrathful skipper ...

That was anaphora. Do you remember Blake's rhetorical questions?

What the hammer? what the chain?
In what furnace was thy brain?
What the anvil? what dread grasp
Dare its deadly terrors clasp?

That was anaphora too. Do you remember the progressio of Ecclesiastes? That was anaphora.

A time to be born, and a time to die; a time to plant, and a time to pluck up that which is planted; A time to kill, and a time to heal; a time to break down, and a time to build up; A time to weep, and a time to laugh; a time to mourn, and a time to dance

And I suppose there is a time to conclude.

Peroration

Shakespeare even told us how to use the figures: 'And practise rhetoric in your common talk.' We do, anyway, to some extent. There is no figure that I've written up here, that you have not, at some time, used. This book is only a looking glass, in which you can see the best of your words.

The aim of this book has been to make clear what is done, a clarity and knowledge that has been abandoned for a couple of centuries now. It is as though we had decided to forget about structural engineering, and instead build our buildings by chance. Any figure overused, or used in the wrong place and at the wrong time, will be a fault. But a figure used and used well, is the beauty of the English language.

Above all, I hope I have dispelled the bleak and imbecilic idea that the aim of writing is to express yourself clearly in plain, simple English using as few words as possible. This is a fiction, a fib, a fallacy, a fantasy and a falsehood. To write for mere utility is as foolish as to dress for mere utility. Mountaineers do it, and climb Everest in clothes that would have you laughed out of the gutter. I suspect they also communicate quickly and efficiently, poor things. But for the rest of us, not threatened by death and yetis, clothes and language can be things of beauty. I would no more write without art because I didn't need to, than I would wander outdoors naked just because it was warm enough. Again.

These figures grow like wildflowers, but they can be cultivated too. I do not believe that The Beatles had any idea what anadiplosis was, any more than I believe that the Rolling Stones knew about syllepsis. They knew what worked, and it did.

The figures of rhetoric are the beauties of all the poems we have ever read. Without them we would merely be us: eating, sleeping, manufacturing and dying. With them everything can be glorious. For though we have nothing to say, we can at least say it well.

Epilogue Concerning Terminology

Rhetorical terminology is a catastrophe and a mess.

Rhetoric was invented by the Ancient Greeks, who thought up lots of lovely Ancient Greek words for the patterns they'd found. But different writers defined these words a little differently. Some used them loosely, some very precisely and some used them with a different meaning altogether.

Then came the Romans. Sometimes they used the Greek terms, and sometimes they thought up their own. And then they got all muddled and used the words in different ways or didn't define them properly at all.

Then came the medieval monks, each sitting in a different monastery, each reading and adapting different Greek and Roman books on rhetoric and muddling things still further.

Then came the Renaissance. Everybody started rediscovering Ancient Rhetoric and adapting it to their own language, even if it didn't fit properly. Puttenham and Peacham and other people beginning with P produced dictionaries of rhetoric in English, which weren't quite the same as the Ancients', but were sort of good enough.

To solve this almighty muddle Puttenham decided to invent a whole new batch of English terms with lovely names like 'the cuckoo-spell' and 'the slow return'. They didn't catch on, and modern books on rhetoric sneer and chortle at him, which is quite unfair.

Usually, this sort of thing got straightened out in the nineteenth and twentieth centuries when the great reference works started to be written. But unfortunately that was the time when rhetoric was out of fashion, and thus the confusion only got confused further. The *Oxford Dictionary of Literary Terms* and the *Oxford English Dictionary* have completely different definitions of zeugma.

The result of all this is that every technical rhetorical term has had fourteen different definitions, and that every figure of rhetoric has had fourteen different names. The standard modern dictionary of rhetoric – Lanham's *A Handlist of Rhetorical Terms* – makes a point of listing all of the alternative names, and all the alternative meanings. If you want to be absolutely sure of the terminology, you should burn this book, and buy Lanham.

This is not a dictionary of rhetoric, nor was it meant to be.

There's also the problem that the lines between this historical figure and that are often very blurry. Careful readers may have noticed that diacope (Crisis? What crisis?) is very similar to epanalepsis (beginning and ending a sentence with the same word), and that epanalepsis is closely related to chiasmus (symmetrical sentence structure) and so on and so forth. Epizeuxis (repeating the same word) is necessarily alliterative and pleonastic and ...

You get the picture, and it ain't a pretty one.

However, it's a truth of all the humanities that you have to learn the distinctions first, and only then can you learn why the distinctions don't really exist. Therefore, I've kept everything in its own little chapter away from its relatives, and given each thing one name.

The purpose of this book has been to show how rhetoric is used in English. Each chapter has tried to identify a figure and illustrate what effect it has using famous examples from the last 500 years. Each one has been given a name that just about fits, but a rose that is called henprosoparapanadiploeia is a rose is a rose is a rose.

However, there are stern and serious scholars who try to sort out this jungle. There are those who would snort at my definition of subjectio, fly into a rage over my views of syllepsis, and, upon reading my definition of scesis onomaton would actually write a letter. Indeed, it occurs to me, dear reader, that you may actually be one of those stern and serious scholars. It's possible. If you are, I would be delighted *never* to hear from you. Seriously. Take that letter, roll it up, wrap it in brambles, and stick it somewhere that alliter... [continued in Chapter 1].

Selected Further Reading

A Handlist of Rhetorical Terms – Richard A. Lanham
(the standard reference work)

Shakespeare's Use of the Arts of Language – Sister Miriam Joseph
(not with a bang but a wimple)

Classical Rhetoric in English Poetry – Professor Sir Brian Vickers
(an excellent introduction)

In Defence of Rhetoric – Professor Sir Brian Vickers
(a comprehensive vindication)

You Talkin' To Me? – Sam Leith (an introduction to the more
structural aspects of rhetoric and persuasion, as opposed to
the verbal figures found here)

And on the internet

Silva Rhetoricae (rhetoric.byu.edu), produced by Gideon O.
Burton of Brigham Young University (a dictionary listing
alternative names and definitions in which one can click
happily between related terms)

The Etymologicon

A Circular Stroll Through the Hidden Connections of the English Language

The *Sunday Times* Number One Bestseller

'I'm hooked on Forsyth's book … Crikey, but this is addictive'
—Matthew Parris, *The Times*

What is the actual connection between *disgruntled* and *gruntled*?
What links church organs to organised crime, California to the
Caliphate, or brackets to codpieces?

As heard on BBC Radio 4, *The Etymologicon* – which springs
from Mark Forsyth's Inky Fool blog – is an occasionally ribald,
frequently witty and unerringly erudite guided tour of the
secret labyrinth that lurks beneath the English language. It takes
in monks and monkeys, film buffs and buffaloes, and explains
precisely what the Rolling Stones have to do with gardening.

ISBN 978-178578-170-4

£8.99

The Horologicon

A Day's Jaunt Through the Lost Words of the English Language

'A magical new book ... Forsyth unveils a selection of obsolete, but oh-so-wonderful words'—*Daily Mail*

'*The Horologicon* lists many of the fabulous, obsolete gems of our language'—Carol Midgley, *The Times*

As heard on BBC Radio 4, *The Horologicon* (or book of hours) gives you the most extraordinary words in the English language, arranged according to the hour of the day when you really need them.

From Mark Forsyth, author of the bestselling *The Etymologicon*, this is a book of weird words for familiar situations. From *ante-jentacular* to *snudge* by way of *quafftide* and *wamblecropt*, at last you can say, with utter accuracy, exactly what you mean.

ISBN 978-178578-171-1

£8.99

The Unknown Unknown
Bookshops and the Delight of Not Getting What You Wanted

Mark Forsyth reveals in this essay, specially commissioned for Independent Booksellers Week, the most valuable thing about a really good bookshop.

Along the way he considers the wisdom of Donald Rumsfeld, naughty French photographs, why Elizabeth Bennet and Mr Darcy would never have met online, and why only a bookshop can give you that precious thing – what you never knew you were looking for.

£1.99 • A6-size paperback • ISBN 978-184831-784-0